Praise for *Po*

"Najah Lightfoot invokes the spir desses—both mythological and re —to guide you through any challenges life might be throwing your way. *Powerful Juju* is packed chock full of tips to bring your magic to life, drawing on strength, courage, and power. With her chapter-by-chapter playlist for the magical soul, Najah takes us on a journey through rite and ritual, walking side by side with strong female figures... No matter what your background may be, *Powerful Juju* has something for everyone, and Najah Lightfoot has created a magical masterpiece."

—Patti Wigington, author of *Herb Magic, Witchcraft for Healing,* and *Badass Ancestors*

"A revolutionary guide through modern magick where Najah Lightfoot guides the reader to power and beauty in the spaces they travel, uncovering Magick in the everyday. Najah provides a proverbial, and sometimes literal, crossroads within its pages. This book is an invaluable tool for Witches of every path and experience level."

—Courtney Weber, author of *Hekate: Goddess of Witches*

"With this latest book, you hold in your hands an intricate cord connecting you back to the deepest wisdom, all through the loving hands of Najah as she deftly braids the four strands of goddess, music, rituals, and her personal tales of what it means to be a witch... You'll be delighted by the pantheon of goddesses that she reveals, one for each chapter. Some are traditional and well-known deities from around the world, others are goddesses that once had human form on this earth and whose legends make them larger than life…This book is destined to be one you return to again and again for spiritually navigating the ups and downs of life—moving through good times and bad with magical grace and ease."

—Madame Pamita, author of *Baba Yaga's Book of Witchcraft* and *The Book of Candle Magic*

"A potent blend of the magick of music and the feminine divine, *Powerful Juju* is a book of uplifting power, suitable for novices and adepts alike. Najah Lightfoot has crafted a unique book, filled with accessible, original spells and rituals, as well as good practical advice for wellbeing and living your best magickal life. *Powerful Juju* makes my heart sing. Highly recommended!"

—Judika Illes, author of *Encyclopedia of 5000 Spells*

"Exploring the power of music and magic, Lightfoot's newest tome is a heady, healing mixtape of grounding rituals and wise and intimate guidance. Drawing upon the potent spells of creativity, art and the history of the empowered feminine, Lightfoot offers up all her title promises—comfort, guidance and fierce protection—brewing up an effective potion for restoration and transformation in these cathartic times."

—Jessica Hundley, author and editor for The Library of Esoterica encyclopedia series

POWERFUL
juju

About the Author

Najah Lightfoot is a multi-award-winning author. She is the author of the bestselling *Good Juju: Mojos, Rites & Practices for the Magical Soul*. She is a regular contributor to the Llewellyn annuals and a contributor to *The Library of Esoterica—Volume III—Witchcraft*. Her magickal staff is on display and part of the permanent collection of the Buckland Museum of Witchcraft, located in Cleveland, Ohio. Najah is a fellow of the Sojourner Truth Leadership Circle, sponsored by Auburn Seminary. She lives in Denver, Colorado, where the blue skies and the power of the Rocky Mountains uplift and fill her soul.

To Write the Author

If you wish to contact the author or would like more information about this book, please write to the author in care of Llewellyn Worldwide, and we will forward your request. Both the author and publisher appreciate hearing from you and learning of your enjoyment of this book and how it has helped you. Llewellyn Worldwide cannot guarantee that every letter written to the author can be answered, but all will be forwarded. Please write to:

Najah Lightfoot
℅ Llewellyn Worldwide
2143 Wooddale Drive
Woodbury, MN 55125.2989

Please enclose a self-addressed stamped envelope for reply, or $1.00 to cover costs. If outside the USA, enclose an international postal reply coupon.

POWERFUL

juju

Goddesses,
Music
& Magic
for Comfort,
Guidance
& Protection

NAJAH LIGHTFOOT

Llewellyn Publications
Woodbury, Minnesota

FIRST EDITION
First Printing, 2022

Book design: Samantha Peterson
Cover design: Kevin R. Brown

Llewellyn Publications is a registered trademark of Llewellyn Worldwide Ltd.

Library of Congress Cataloging-in-Publication Data (Pending)
ISBN: 978-0-7387-6715-4

Llewellyn Publications
A Division of Llewellyn Worldwide Ltd.
2143 Wooddale Drive
Woodbury, MN 55125.2989
www.llewellyn.com

Printed in the United States of America

This book is dedicated to the Goddess,
in all her names, images, and personifications.
She who shall not be denied or forgotten.

contents

acknowledgments

THIS BOOK WOULD NOT have been possible without the support and encouragement of the following people, places, and things.

My family: my husband, Tim Bagley; our son, Robert P. Herrmann; and our daughter, Kelly Bagley.

Kara Seal, who is my awesome writer buddy; Elysia Gallo; Stephanie Finne; and the wonderful team and staff at Llewellyn. Melanie Marquis, author extraordinaire and friend.

Many thanks to Lois Harvey and Matt Aragon-Shafi of Westside Books; Lisa Anderson, Courtney Weber Hoover, and my sisters of the Sojourner Truth Leadership Circle; Toni Rotonda (thanks for all the magickal phone calls), Steven Intermill, and the Buckland Museum of Witchcraft and Magick; Gretchen and Richard Ashburn; Sallie Ann Glassman and Amy Hession; Mary Ann Bonetti, Taylor Mareah, Colleen Ring, Tiffany Boggins of Witchlab, Erika Fortner (Queen Meb), Bevin Antea, Kate Antea, Cheryl Stratten, and Sará Rain; the American Southwest, *That Witch Life* podcast, and the Doreen Valiente Foundation; and Jake-Ryan Kent at Llewellyn, who gave me the most powerful reading I've ever had. To all my true followers and friends on Instagram, Twitter, Facebook, and YouTube, your encouragement and support to write a second book means so much to me!

My spiritual guides: Mama Marie Laveau and Aunt Clara. My sweet dog, Terra, who lies at my feet when I write, and the birds who come to my bird feeder. Colorado sunrises, starry skies at night, and countless hours of music, which soothes, inspires, and uplifts me.

introduction

Song: **"Couldn't Stand the Weather"**
Artist: **Stevie Ray Vaughan**

WELCOME TO *POWERFUL JUJU: Goddesses, Music & Magic for Comfort, Guidance & Protection*, which builds on the magickal and spiritual foundation laid in my book *Good Juju: Mojos, Rites & Practices for the Magical Soul.* In this book, you will find powerful rites and rituals designed to aid you when life gets tough and heavy-handed, for surely each of us has our own burdens to bear.

We all have times when we feel alone, powerless, angry, scared, and hopeless. *Powerful Juju* introduces you to twelve goddesses: mythological, real, and contemporary women whose lives stood the test of time through countless ordeals of pain and suffering and who triumphed into beings we can look to for help, guidance, and assistance. They offer their stories as testaments of strength, power, and courage.

The myths and true lives of these women affect us. They call to us from the Ether and the great beyond. They rise up as great vines, snarling, twisting, clawing their way through the cracks of time, into the Universe of our daily lives. We can turn to these magnificent souls for inspiration, comfort, guidance, and protection. We can touch our hearts to their spirits through the realms of prayer, magick, and ritual.

There were songs that inspired me as I wrote this book. Songs that keep me going when things get too tough to bear, times when I've found myself in the crossroads of life and asking for help. Just because I am a magickal, spiritual person, that doesn't mean I get a free pass! Actually, it seems my heart gets worked over even harder! The songs will help you dive deep into this book as you read and work through each chapter. Listen, and allow the music to bring you deeper into the crossroads of magick, powerful healing, and deep juju.

Rise Up

I'm a city girl. I was born in Cleveland, Ohio, and raised on the West Coast in the city of the angels: Los Angeles, California. I grew up wearing hot pants, going to the beach, listening to Michael Jackson, dancing, poppin' my fingers, and groovin' to the songs of the '60s and '70s. Magic was in the air and in the music. Spells were cast over the radio and through the speakers of our home stereo.

My family moved from Ohio to LA to San Diego, California, and then to Colorado Springs, Colorado, in 1977. Talk about an upheaval of mind, body, and soul! Since that time, I have called Colorado my home, moving to Denver in 1985.

I make no claims. I only know what is true and authentic for me. I know songs heal, fellowship is important, and the sharing of truth is powerful. I know it can be hard to rise up when you feel the world is against you. It can be hard to turn your face to the sun and appreciate a new day when all you feel or see is darkness. It can be hard to believe good is coming, hope is around the corner, or times will change, especially when so much to the contrary tries to convince you to give up, that there is no reason for you to believe your sorrows will be lessened, or that you can have a good day.

Working and changing your sorrows into joy takes time. It's hard. Darkness likes darkness. It doesn't want you to shine that light upon it. It wants to grab hold of you, smother you, choke you. The less light you shine upon it, the stronger it grows.

We're not here to ignore our sorrows or magickally wish them away. We're here to do the work. We're here to rise up. We're here to honor our scabby knees and broken hearts, to empty that box of tissue and then another, until we don't need that tissue anymore. We're here to light the fucking candle, put a flame to our sorrows. We're here to call upon the power of the Divine Feminine, stand in the crossroads, and raise our arms to the sky.

We're here to strengthen and help each other get up. That's right. I said, "Get up."

I know you may not want to. Hell, there've been many times when I didn't want to get out of bed. Why bother?

There's been many a day when I've felt this world sucks and it seems the nasty people always win.

But we can't stay in that place; it's not good for us. I know it's exhausting. We get so gawd damn tired. Yet, maybe, through the pages of this book, with the assistance of twelve badass goddesses, through these kickass songs that help us rise up, we can get up, together.

Worthy of the Title "Goddess"

Goddess. Divine Feminine. Great Mother. She of many names. I have the strength of ten thousand women!

Some of the women I refer to as "goddesses" actually lived and breathed upon the physical plane. What all the legendary women listed in my book have in common, whether they be real or mythological, is the true *essence* of a goddess. They are brilliant, inspiring women.

These iconic women give us something to strive toward, someone to look up to, something to grab and hold tight. Whether they were real or mythological women, they stood up for their truth and left their mark upon the world in story, in art, through enslavement, in song, in magick, in spirituality. They left a path for us to follow and examples to turn to when our lives become complicated or the burden becomes too heavy to bear.

Lilith, the magnificent winged one, whose clawed feet grab hold and won't let go. In this book, we call upon Lilith for strength.

Frida Kahlo, the incomparable artist and goddess of triumph, who inspires us to carry on through her unflinching art and unwavering sense of style—including her unibrow, which has taken on feminist icon status, yet is a common feature on the faces of many women in Mexico. We call on Frida Kahlo for overcoming pain.

The Divine Marie Laveau: New Orleans icon, Lwa of New Orleans Vodou, Hoodoo magick, Woman of Color, powerful, mysterious, and giving. No matter how many pictures, portraits, or artistic renderings of Mama Marie (a term of endearment I call her) there may be, it has been well documented that she never sat for a painting. Her true likeness was never captured on canvas. All we have of her is what an artist *thought* she may have looked like, granting her the artist's ideas of beauty and stature. However, whoever takes on the task of painting Marie Laveau's portrait, they give her eyes that blaze into your soul. We seek Marie Laveau for comfort in our times of need, especially during court cases.

Manman Brijit, goddess of the cemetery, will listen to your petition. I take her image from the *New Orleans Voodoo Tarot Deck*. Manman Brijit sits upon her pyramid of stones in her garment of the deceased, staring out of fathomless eyes. We go to Manman Brijit in the cemetery to support our court case work that may lead to jail time.

Sekhmet: old, ancient, and wise. Sekhmet, crowned in her lion headdress, forces you to look away. She is formidable and dares you to look her in the face. We beseech Sekhmet for power.

Tituba, an enslaved Woman of Color, is heroic and deserving of recognition. Tituba, of whom there are no pictures, only drawings, wore the rags of an enslaved woman. We can easily imagine her in tatters with her head tied up. We ask Tituba to help us be ourselves.

Sulis Minerva is goddess of ancient and deep waters. Sulis Minerva has strong, commanding features and a look that could lead warriors into battle. We go to Sulis Minerva for healing.

Nina Simone: Black Woman, classically trained soul singer, icon, and revolutionary. Nina Simone had strong, powerful, striking features, which made her instantly recognizable. We go to Nina Simone to welcome new beginnings.

Nancy Wilson: African American woman; icon of suave, smooth, and sultry grace. Nancy Wilson makes you check your clothes and asks you, "Are you really going out in *that*?" We cry with the legendary jazz singer Nancy Wilson when our hearts are broken.

Abundantia is the Roman goddess of prosperity. Abundantia's face gazes over her cornucopia, her face rendered by the artistic hands of Roman times. We find prosperity with Abundantia.

Sybil Leek is the British Witch of powerful vision. Sybil Leek was as solid as a woman can be. We touch insight and self-reflect with Sybil Leek.

Doreen Valiente, Mother Witch to the modern movement of Witchcraft, towered in her spirituality as the Mother of Witches. We find the ability to carry on with Doreen Valiente.

All these women stand out from the crowd. They refuse to be put in a box, categorized, or rendered useless by arcane standards. They have all left their marks upon the Universe and the doorways of time. They will not be silenced by those who do not understand, are not enlightened, or misjudge their true character and worth. When weary, we can call to these women, turn to them, offer our tears and supplications for mercy unto them. It is for these reasons these iconic women listed in my book are worthy of the title "goddess."

The Music

I've loved music since childhood. If I love a song, I'll wear it out. I can play the same song over and over and over again. Prior to music playing in our heads through AirPods, headphones, or Bluetooth connections, I would blast my musical crushes through my speakers at ear-damaging decibels.

The musicians understood me.

How can it be that a song, heard at just the right time, can ease my pain, lift my soul? But it does. Music does exactly that. Perhaps that's why some of us lose ourselves in the rhythm, wait for days to see our favorite bands, or read everything we can get our hands on about our favorite musicians.

When I hear a fiddle play or fingers scraping over a washboard through the sounds of folk or root music, something way down deep in my soul wakes up and calls my name. It's a haunting feeling, one I can't escape. I have visions of dirt floors, a porch with a jug on it, a garden growing vegetables and flowers, all surrounded by tall green trees. I can hear the lonesome tune of a banjo and smell the smoke from a corncob pipe and the scent of a rich stew cooking over a crackling fire.

I *know* this music. I've always had a deep connection to the past. What's even crazier is I didn't grow up listening to this type of music. My childhood home was mostly filled with jazz and R&B, which gave me a substantial appreciation for rhythm and blues, harmonies and melodies.

Although I'm not a musician, my ear and my soul love bluegrass, folk music, and mountain music, as well as popular and contemporary tunes. There has been many a time when I've been the only Black girl at a bluegrass festival. But I didn't care. I love this music. It fills me and soothes me, which is one of the reasons I lost my mind when I learned about zydeco music. I couldn't get over the fact that there are Black people wearing cowboy hats, swinging, and dancing their hearts out!

Yes, there's some Creole down in my soul, too. When that fiddle gets going or the strings of a banjo start strumming and the wailing voices begin, I find myself drawn to the crossroads at night or to the graveyard to cry and wash away my sorrows. I recognize it. I hear it. I feel it. This root music calls me to honor my ancestors. It calls me through the mighty ceremonies and Master Drummers of New Orleans Vodou. It makes me chant and sing in the cold frigid hours of morning, on the steps of Red Rocks Amphitheatre, along with hundreds of kindred souls, as we honor and welcome the Winter Solstice.

This music also drives me to practice magick, write spells, and write books. It fuels my prayers so that my words will help just one person who longs to find a better and more powerful way to ease their troubles when the heavy weather comes down. Because down it does come. To be human is not only to experience joy, but also to experience sorrow. It is the yin and yang of life.

One day, I was sitting in a bar. My heart was heavy. Something that had troubled my mind and heart had reared up and shown its ugly head, once again. This wasn't a new issue, but the pain I was feeling was a new level of emotion. I was weary. It was daylight, but the skies were dark. A cold drizzle was falling. The shadow of defeat and exhaustion hung heavy on my shoulders.

The bartender, a sweet person, someone very dear to me, poured me a drink. It was some type of relieving concoction, which I immediately drank. I felt better, but something was missing.

I didn't realize, that day when I was deep in my woes, that you could access a digital jukebox. I grew up in the time of jukeboxes, turntables, and record players. I grew up going to the record store to buy vinyl records, albums, and cassettes.

The bartender was kind enough to school me. As I sat in the quiet bar, my fingers scrolling through the digital selections, I found Stevie Ray Vaughan and "Couldn't Stand the Weather."

When the song blasted into the room, the bartender poured me another drink. Heads began nodding, and shoulders swayed a bit as my comrades and I drank our libations while Stevie Ray burned up his guitar strings with his magical fingers. In the dimly lit room, as I sipped my drink and listened to Stevie's blues, I felt a healing come over me.

The music. It knew my pain. I must have listened to that song twenty times that day, and thus the impetus for this book was born.

Music is healing. Music is personal, music is intimate. We might not relate to everyone's favorite singer, band, or song, but we get why they like it. Music is transcendent. And when you find the right groove, you can truly get over the rainbow.

This book seeks to bring you into the groove of songs that capture my heart, lift my soul, and spur me onward. The songs in the playlist for the goddesses are also sung by women. Women whose voices touch our hearts and souls. Women who uplift us, comfort us, and strengthen us through their exceptional talent and artistry.

The entire playlist is listed in the appendix. All the songs are available via the Powerful Juju Playlist on streaming music media; however, the best way to listen to the playlist is on You-Tube: "Powerful Juju ~ Najah Lightfoot ~ Author." You can listen to all the songs in the playlist before reading a word. However, I *encourage* you to read the book in chapter order and listen to each song as you go, allowing your mind and spirit to be soothed and uplifted.

How to Use This Book

Grab your headphones, AirPods, or Bluetooth speakers and turn them up, loud. Together, through the pages of this book, you and I will get in a groove. We shall face the stormy times with faith and magick, which I pray will be a guide and a lift to you.

Each goddess was chosen to help with a different condition in your life, each one selected for her powerful juju to help you overcome troubled times that may be sapping your strength, marring your spiritual vision, bringing you down, or affecting your ability to be strong and carry on. Each goddess chapter begins with why I chose that goddess and includes a bit of her background and why she can be called on.

Following the goddess sections are the soul speak sections. They were inspired, written as I tuned in to each woman, listening deeply to the music for that chapter. Sometimes the words that poured forth from my heart read as a poem, or, as I like to call it, "tuning in" to Spirit.

Each chapter includes a rite or ritual that can be used to call upon the goddess, which can be worked at your own pace to bring you into closer relationship with that particular goddess. As you feel more comfortable doing the work, you can work the rites as you need them. The sacred spaces sections offer suggestions for creating touchstone spaces for each goddess should you wish to bring her spirituality into your life on a regular and consistent basis.

You can always start small. There is no need to try to do all the rituals and rites listed in this book at once. Read the text many times. Get comfortable with the instructions. Download the playlist and listen to the music. Sit and be with the songs and their lyrics. Let their powerful juju stir in your mind for a while. Then return to these pages when the time comes for you to put what you have learned into action.

A note on my spelling of the word *magick*. As a novice Witch, I was taught that spelling the word *magic* with a *k* differentiates it from the use of magic as a sleight of hand performance—something stage magicians would do to entertain an audience—and the use for people, specifically students of the Occult, who use magic(k) intentionally, as in rites, spells, and rituals to effect change in their lives. Since this book intentionally focuses on rites and rituals to effect positive change—to uplift, heal, and comfort—in several chapters, you will find *magic* spelled with a *k*.

If the word is spelled *magic*, I am speaking about emotions and feelings. If it is spelled *magick*, I am speaking about working rites and rituals with focused intention.

Now, let us journey to the crossroads to wade through and emerge from the dark of troubling times. May your goddesses, gods, angels, deities, and Higher Powers be with you, for none of us need stand or walk alone. We need the help of each other and Spirit. Embrace the starry night of sleep and wonder and fuel our magical souls to keep going, one day and one night at a time. Together, we can do the work and perform the rites and rituals to help us smile in the morning sun.

one
doing the work

Song: "Darlin' Cory"
Artist: Amythyst Kiah

I'VE NEVER CONSIDERED MYSELF an activist, yet I suppose in my own way, I am. I suppose if I was looking for a label, I would say I am a spiritual activist, one who believes in the power of women, the strength of a Higher Power, and the mysteries of the Universe. One who believes we need examples of courage, the ability to overcome, the ability to go the distance to achieve our goals, dreams, wishes, and desires.

Personally, I align with the word *Witch*. Maybe you do, too, and if you don't, that's okay. We all move at our own speed and development.

I embrace and reclaim the word *Witch* for its strong feminine power. I have always been drawn to working with the Divine Feminine and spiritual practices that support my journey. The word *Witch*, however, is gender neutral. What matters is, if you choose to align with *Witch*, do so from a place of reverence, respect, and remembrance for those who have gone before you.

In the history of the Craft, we could not always speak openly about our practices, and for some people, that freedom is still not a possibility. Many people still face harassment for openly declaring their beliefs or practices. Many people can't speak publicly about being a Witch or their interests in the Occult. It may not be safe for them, their children, their family, or their employment. We must use discernment with our voices. Knowing how and when to speak up is a valuable tool.

We are still very young in our journey with Witchcraft in the history of the modern world. We, too, are creating new ways and paths for others to follow. As the Craft of the Wise continues to evolve, some practices will be discarded, and new ones will take their place. We should seek to be inclusive and not exclusive.

For those seeking to work powerful juju, time, effort, and dedication are a must. In my humble opinion, being a Witch is more than just having the ability to download spells and read books; it is the ability to *practice*. Have you ever wondered why it is called the Craft?

A craft is something you learn and study. It grows and develops as you put time and effort into it. As you gain strength, power, and confidence, so does your Craft. I know this not only from the many years I have spent in ritual, doing spell work and rites, but also from my time spent studying martial arts.

I like to say, "I'm a simple Witch," which is not to be confused with "simpleminded"! Although I know complicated rites and practices, I tend to work magick that is easily performed, doesn't require many items, and is something I can do anywhere. I'm that magickal person who has done a few things a thousand times. I have great magickal muscle memory. Which I hope you will develop, too.

If you put in the time and effort, you will develop magickal muscle memory. You will begin to align with what works for you, things that bring a sense of harmony and well-being, and rites and rituals that feel good to you when you do them.

A Few Words on Working with the Lwa of Vodou/New Orleans Vodou

Vodou is a *religion*. It requires commitment, time and effort, and practice. It requires initiation to become a member of a Vodou House or Society, which is similar to being baptized or christened in a mainstream faith or organized religion.

So, while I have shared rites and rituals that call upon working with the Lwa, doing them does not make you an initiate of Vodou. For that, you need the guidance, blessing, and initiation from a Manbo/Mambo or Oungan/Houngan who are leaders of their respective Vodou Houses or Societies.

However, you can use these rites to draw you deeper into relationship with the Lwa, which may in time lead you to *desire* initiation into the religion of Vodou.

There is a difference between Hoodoo and Vodou. The knowledge and practices of Hoodoo can be gained from many different sources. You can learn it from your aunties, various teachers, online courses, books, and workshops. But to immerse yourself properly in the religion of Vodou, you need the guidance of a Manbo/Mambo or Oungan/Houngan, who have spent years in service to the Lwa, and who have also received the level of initiation to carry those titles.

So don't get it twisted.

Hoodoo is primarily an African American Folk Magick tradition. Practicing Hoodoo is learning and using the practices of a Folk Magick tradition. *Vodou is a religion.* It is a way of faith and practice, which for many takes years before they realize they are ready to commit to the path of initiation. Initiation requires vows. As you work with these rites for Manman Brijit and Marie Laveau, you may feel the urge for further study and connection with those who initiated into Vodou.

A step into initiation for any spiritual or religious calling should be done with sincere soul-searching and time spent with your Higher Power, deities, goddesses, and gods. One step can lead to another.

Circle Casting

"To cast or not to cast? That is the question!"

You will notice most of the rituals and rites I have written in this book do not require you to cast a circle. Casting a circle is a rite of Witchcraft that at one time or another most Witches will perform, either as a solitary Witch or in the company of other Witches, as a way to perform magick, honor the seasons, or keep the full moon. However, casting a circle is not a requirement for being a Witch!

With that said, should you desire to learn to cast a circle, I go into great detail for a proper casting in my chapter dedicated to Doreen Valiente. A few tidbits I have learned in my many years of casting circles are the following: make sure you have everything handy before you begin, always have a backup lighter or matches, take a shower or bath before you begin (or give yourself a quick wash from a sink, if you don't have time to shower or bathe), and try to cast your circle when you will not be disturbed. Lastly and most importantly, go easy on yourself when you first begin. Distractions will happen, you'll forget stuff, or the weather or timing may not cooperate. Just keep going, and soon you'll be a proficient Witch who can cast a circle!

Petition Papers

A petition paper is a note you write to Spirit, stating your intentions. It is your opportunity to state as clearly as possible, in your own words, your desires and wishes. The act of writing out your intentions is the manifestation and visualization of what lies in your mind and heart into matter. It is the magickal dynamic that occurs between the mind, your spirit, the ink, the pen, and the paper.

I was taught to use brown paper torn from a brown paper bag, with no machine-created sides. This means tearing each side of the paper so the paper is jagged on all four sides. When you have finished tearing your paper, write your prayers for courage, strength, and confidence. Anoint the paper with five drops of olive oil in a five-spot pattern: place a drop of olive oil in the upper left corner of the paper, then continue clockwise, placing a drop in all four corners. Finish by placing a drop of olive oil in the center of the paper.

We will use petition papers in the rites for Sekhmet and Abundantia.

Florida Water

Contrary to popular belief, Florida Water is not made in Florida. *Agua de florida* means "waters of flowers." Florida Water is available in brick-and-mortar metaphysical stores, spiritual botanicas, and online shops that sell spiritual supplies. I use Florida Water in most of the goddess rituals in this book, so be sure to have some on hand.

Florida Water is one of the most popular items used in Hoodoo and magickal spell work. Many people may be familiar with Florida Water from its time-honored spot on the drugstore shelf next to witch hazel. For nearly two hundred years, Florida Water has been used as a cooling, healing remedy for the skin, as a refreshing addition to your bathwater after a long hot day, or as a spicy citrus cologne that cleanses and uplifts the body, mind, and spirit.

However, where Florida Water really shines is in the spiritual realm. Shamans, Witches, healers, and all types of practitioners swear by Florida Water for its ability to clear negative energy, attract good luck, and protect one from nightmares,

and its use as an offering to your ancestors. As a spiritual blessing in liquid form, it can anoint one's body daily to keep the
good and powerful juju flowing all around.

Although homemade recipes abound, the most famous and
easily found version of Florida Water is made by Murray &
Lanman. Their bottle of Florida Water is easily recognizable
by its long neck, foil wrapping, and lovely imagery of flowers,
birds, and a flowing waterfall on the label.

You will notice Florida Water often being used in this
book to cleanse candles before rituals. To cleanse a candle, use
the Florida Water to wipe from the center upward toward the
wick and from the center downward toward the base. If you
are using a tealight, wipe the top of the candle with Florida
Water.

"Darlin' Cory" ~ Crossroads and Graveyards

In the song "Darlin' Cory," Amythyst Kiah's voice resonates
across time. It is time to dig a hole so we can lay Darlin' Cory
down. I heard Amythyst Kiah sing this song at Swallow Hill
Music Hall in my hometown of Denver, Colorado, in 2019.
When she played her banjo and sang her truth, I was transported to another place and time. She stood on the stage
alone, accompanied only by her banjo and guitar. This incredible Black Woman put a healing on my soul. She brought me
home.

See, sometimes, we've got to lay our troubles down. I
know about trouble. I know about wailing in the graveyard,
and I know about burying things in graveyards. I know about

creeping out at the midnight hour to touch with ancestors and benevolent spirits for help. Sometimes I've gone alone, and sometimes I was accompanied by my sweet familiar dog, who stood guard.

If you're going to the crossroads or graveyard, the agreement you must enter into is that this work is never to be taken irreverently or lightly. Also, not all cemeteries allow people to leave offerings on a gravesite. Be sure to check the rules and regulations before you do your work in a graveyard. It is up to you and your Higher Power to decide to move forward with working in a graveyard. Once you decide, you've got to be sure. You've got to commit.

Before you decide, have you prayed about it? Have you asked your Higher Power, creator, gods, and goddesses for guidance? Have you had an inner conversation with yourself about why you're about to do this type of work?

Did you read all the steps and visualize yourself doing these acts? Did it feel good? Did you feel empowered? Or did you feel scared, nervous, and not quite sure?

It's okay to feel nervous; that just means you're getting ready. Feeling scared and not quite ready is different. Maybe you should give the work you're about to do a little more thought and time.

These are all the steps you must take before you lay your troubles down at the crossroads or graveyard. Because once you do, you've got to follow the work all the way.

Some of our troubles need to be buried in the ground for us to be free of them. We've got to bury them, cry and wail over them. We have to go out in the night or in the early hours of the morn. And we have to go alone. It can be scary. This work digs into your soul and your fears. That's why we do our inner work first, by praying to our Higher Power, meditating, and consulting tools of divination, such a tarot cards or pendulums.

Once you've finished your work, *hush*—don't tell. Be still with your work until you've safely made it back home. Keep your mouth shut until you know the outcome of your work.

Even after you know the outcome, you may decide to never tell anyone what you've done. You may decide in the long run it's best to keep your work secret, forever inaccessible to all, except to those you've called upon in Spirit for help.

I remember like it was yesterday the first time I went to a graveyard in the middle of the night to dig a hole and lay my troubles down. I had been working my spell for hours. I'd thought I'd be finished by midnight. But the spell had taken way longer than anticipated, and I hadn't set out for the graveyard until after two o'clock in the morning. But I was determined, and my need was great. Serious trouble was brewing. Dark shadows were hovering around someone I love deeply. I didn't know names or faces, but I "knew" they were present. Thankfully, my sweet dog accompanied me. She sat quietly in the car as my watcher while I did my work in the cemetery.

Now, of course, I had done my prep work.

I had driven around the cemetery not once but many times. Those of us who are urban workers have it tough. We don't have access to open, unlocked cemeteries like those you see in small or rural towns. Or, as Amythyst Kiah sings in her song, an open meadow where we can just dig a hole. But that's okay. I find these obstacles just make me a stronger, more capable worker, Witch, practitioner, goddess incarnate, badass woman.

Please note that going to the crossroads or graveyard at midnight can be a daunting experience. Before you attempt any ritual or rite that requires you to leave your home after dark, take proper steps to ensure you are comfortable doing so. In this book, we'll only be visiting the crossroads in a ritual for Lilith and the graveyard in a ritual calling upon Manman Brijit, so if you aren't ready for this kind of work, you'll find plenty of other options to explore.

A few helpful hints:

- Scope out your intended graveyard or crossroads during daylight hours so you are familiar with the surrounding environment.

- Check out the graveyard or crossroads at midnight (using your preferred mode of transportation) before doing your ritual. You will find places look very different at night than they do during the day.

- Tell a trusted friend, partner, spouse, or family member of your intention to go to the graveyard or crossroads at night, if that makes you more comfortable.

- If you feel completely overwhelmed by performing a midnight graveyard or crossroads ritual, wait and give yourself some time to decide if it is the right ritual for you.

Preparing for the Rites

The rites in this book may cause you to step out of your comfort zone. If you're a seasoned practitioner, it may be only a matter of tuning in to your magickal self before you begin the work. If you're a beginner, you may need to go slow and easy before you feel ready. Whichever way you decide to move forward in doing the ritual work is fine. This work is helping you become better acquainted with magick and powerful juju. However, I do have a few suggestions to help you when you are ready to perform the rites and rituals listed in this book:

- As you prepare for your rite, read through the entire text before you begin your work. Listen to the suggested song for the goddess you will call upon to aid you.

- Tune in to your gut, your feelings, and your emotions. How do you feel when you visualize yourself doing the rite you are reading? Do you feel a sense of relief? Do you feel you will gain something positive by doing this work? Do you feel this magickal work will be a boost to your confidence? This is the inner journey you must take, for all magick begins in our minds and spirit.

- If you feel a sense of foreboding or deep anxiety, this may not be the right time for you to do this work. It's okay to take a step back and rethink your intentions.

- Many times our intuition or gut will give us answers. If the instructions call for you to step into the crossroads at midnight, drive by your chosen crossroads at midnight *before* your ritual. If the instructions call for you to be somewhere at the crack of dawn, go check that place out at the crack of dawn *before* you do your ritual.

- Real magick takes time and effort. Real magick, powerful juju, takes time and preparation. If you're not serious about it, I suggest you reconsider your intentions, or if this is something you can really do. And don't take the chickenshit way out either by hiring someone else to do it for you. You want change? You want results? Do the work yourself!

- It takes strength, courage, and power to do these works. It takes alignment and relationship with your Higher Power. Make no mistake—you are entering into work with forces greater than yourself, and it would behoove you to damn well respect them.

- Sacred grounds, graveyards, ancestors, and crossroads do not take lightly to irreverence and disrespect. Show them love. Show them honor. Show them respect, because you may need to return to those places at a future time for help.

A Word to the Wise

The rites and rituals described in this book are in no way intended to substitute the help, guidance, or aid of a professional mental health provider or physician. These are spiritual aids I have found helpful, and they are shared only with the intention to impart spiritual knowledge and experience. If you are in crisis, please consult a doctor or qualified therapist to assist you with your troubles.

Magick, spirituality and science, and licensed, qualified physicians, as well as professional mental health workers and therapists, can and do work magnificently with each other. One need not rule out one modality for another. In fact, the best healing often occurs when a person combines their religion, their spirituality, their magickal practices, *and* the guidance of a licensed health-care professional.

Sankofa

Many of us are empathic, sympathetic, sensitive souls. We feel things deeply. We have no problems walking in another person's shoes, melding our hearts with others, peering deeply into the eyes of a wounded soul, and offering help. These are wonderful qualities, good qualities. It is indeed a good thing to be compassionate, empathize, and have sympathy for another person. For there is evil in this world. Make no mistake about it.

I don't believe in the devil or Satan, but I have seen evil. I have seen it rise up and seek to quell the very breath of life we depend on.

While I was writing this book, millions of people saw evil rise up in the clear light of day. It rose up in the form of a knee pressed upon the neck of a Black Man, an African American man, named George Floyd, and it broke my fucking heart.

This evil rose up in the form of a white man, dressed in the uniform of those who are sworn to serve and protect. The police. And they didn't protect. They killed. They murdered.

And then the young people came. They came with their outrage and their peaceful protests. And we watched them get fired on with tear gas and rubber bullets.

Then there were others who saw an opportunity to usurp the peaceful protests and use this time of anguish, grief, and sorrow for their own sadistic personal gains.

It was hard, difficult, traumatic. Everything we depended on —our prayers, our rites and rituals—seemed lacking. Most days, all I could do was cry.

It wasn't the first time.

These types of malicious and heinous acts have happened throughout history, across the planet, in many places and spaces. However, in the United States, we have yet to find our way out, to finally squash the violent images and acts, which used to appear in newspapers, but now show up on our tablets, computer screens, and iPhones.

But let us not despair. We can learn from these experiences. We can grow. We can become stronger and apply healing to ourselves and our hearts. We can move on, take the pain we've gone through and awake stronger and more capable to face a new day. We can become Sankofa, an African symbol of a bird flying forward with its head turned backward. I wear a copper Sankofa bracelet on my arm. Sankofa is wisdom gained from the past with the courage to fly forward.

Come and be with me as we work powerful juju for troubled times with the assistance of badass goddesses.

two
finding strength
with lilith

Song: "Missionary Man"
Artist: Eurythmics

THERE IS MUCH LORE associated with the Goddess Lilith. She is known as a screech owl, night monster, storm goddess, patroness of Witches, and dark and fearful demon goddess from Jewish folklore. She is one who has been demonized and who inspires fear in the patriarchy.

She is a seductive, enticing sorceress, one with clawed feet. She is in complete control and will not be dominated. She shall not submit, having been banished from history for refusing to lie beneath the biblical Adam during intercourse. Instead, she vanished into the air and was found having sex with demons, creating her own children!

Lilith helps us through dark and troubled times. She is a patron goddess for all who are looking for a symbol of strength and the ability to overcome difficulties. Lilith will not be denied. Wherever she sits or stands, she commands the space.

Lilith doesn't apologize. She doesn't cower. She gives the ultimate finger to the patriarchy! She doesn't respect authority, and she certainly doesn't run from conflict. She embraces her Divine Feminine power and uses it to fly away from those who don't understand her or, worse, seek to persecute her for being herself. Lilith is the ultimate Witch woman goddess.

For so long, women have been told to keep quiet, stay in their lane, not to make too much noise, calm down. Ugh! Lilith is anything but calm. She is a Witch bitch!

Lilith roars out of our collective consciousness that tells us we need to be quiet and submit, to stuff all manner of irrational dogma heaped upon us as sensitive, empathic people. How many times have you felt someone was giving you the evil eye or wasn't telling you the truth? How many times have you tucked your feelings into your downy wings and cried? How many times have you felt alone, misunderstood, or ostracized?

Lilith's wings will carry you to the crossroads if you're brave enough to face those fears at midnight. Lilith is the demon goddess of strength and power; let her lift you up and carry your heartache away. Let her banish those nightmares and hurt feelings. Let her strength be yours until you find your own strength and power.

Deep down in your core, you know you can do this. You know you're ready. It gets tiring, carrying all that heartache around. Lilith can ease your load, empty your satchel of broken promises and lies. She'll listen to you. She won't judge. Remember, she herself was judged and banished. But away she did not go. She rises up out of the darkness of time and calls to those who would honor her, give her her propers, her respect. R.E.S.P.E.C.T.

Soul Speak

Heavy weather. Cat claw scratching. I'm runnin'. Dogs are howling; I can't see. Someone is chasing me—they're after me. I can't breathe. Down on my knees, going to the crossroads, calling out to one who can help me.

Lilith!

Heavy winged one, who refused to lie down, to bow before anyone. My troubles are heavy. I can't bear it no more. Hear my cry. Answer my plea. This terror in my heart is hurting me.

*Rise up, child! Gather your strength. My wings will
protect you. I am not for the meek. Leave it here.
Bear it no more. Get up, girl! Your knees are sore.
Bruised though you may be, I am here for thee.*

Allow Lilith to go with you to the crossroads in the hour of midnight. Allow her power and strength to align with yours as you wash away your fears and stand in strength at the midnight hour in the crossroads!

"Missionary Man" ~ Why I Chose
This Song for Goddess Lilith

In "Missionary Man," Annie Lennox's voice screams at us. In my mind's eye, I can still see Annie in concert at the famous Red Rocks Amphitheatre in Denver, Colorado, back in the 1980s. She was standing on top of a rail in a shiny black leather miniskirt and tank top, whipping the crowd into a frenzy.

It was one of the greatest concerts of my life. There is nothing small, quiet, or submissive about Annie Lennox or this song. And neither is there anything small, quiet, or submissive about the Goddess Lilith. When I sat down to write about Lilith, it was this song that drove me on, made me rise up, and carried me to the crossroads.

Lilith Fair

The Goddess Lilith showed up in my life long before I came to acknowledge her as a powerful Witch. She came into my life at a gathering of strong, inspiring women—led by the musician Sarah McLachlan—known as Lilith Fair, an incredible musical extravaganza.

Lilith Fair came to my hometown of Denver, Colorado, in 1998. At that time, I was working for a battered women's shelter; we were given tickets and invited to participate in the event to support women and provide information and resources for those suffering from domestic violence.

It was a bright, sunny day at Fiddler's Green Amphitheatre. What I remember most is there were women everywhere! We seemed to cover every square inch of the venue, and there was so much excitement and enthusiasm! We all knew we were part of something great.

Though I didn't know much about Sarah McLachlan, I was super excited to see and hear Queen Latifah perform. Yes, indeed; it was a historic event, and I'm glad I was part of it.

I purchased a CD at the event, which had a beautiful green backdrop and an image of Lilith as cover art. Sadly, I played it so many times, I eventually warped and scratched the disk, and I have no idea where the case wound up—but the memory, the power, and the gratitude for that event have stayed with me. Lilith Fair showed me women can do anything! We can pull together and help each other, support each other, and lift each other up, which is why Lilith is the first goddess in this book. Her wings have been beneath me for a very long time, and I pray you, too, will find strength and power in her magick.

I keep a reddish statue of Lilith on my desk. She is fierce in her look as she stands firm upon her platform. Behind her sits a large, extremely dark smoky quartz sphere. My statue of Lilith has large wings. Looking through the space her wings create, I can see the dark smoky quartz sphere. This imagery gives me courage and strength. I can feel Lilith spurring me on, encouraging me to face my fears and emerge triumphant.

Find a Lilith statue and place it on your altar or in a private place where she can bless you with strength! Praise Lilith for her strength, her rebellion, her unwillingness to accept defeat, to be controlled or dominated. Call upon her to release the shackles and chains that bind and torment you.

Take Me to the Crossroads Ritual

This is a powerful ritual to perform when you feel your mind has been clouded by dark thoughts you sense are coming from fear. A long time ago, I learned an acronym for the word *fear*: False Evidence Appearing Real.

It matters not whether your fears are grounded in real experiences or if you just feel haunted or plagued by something you can't quite put your finger on—or maybe you're burdened with guilt. Perhaps guilt is a brick upon your shoulder that is bruising your skin and causing you to look back for the monster of unresolved business. Or maybe you need to make amends to someone, and you're scared to do it.

What matters is these thoughts, real or imagined, are intruders to your peace of mind, your serenity, your confidence, and your courage. In short, they need to be rooted out, destroyed, and sent packing.

Items Needed

  2 white unscented tealights

  Florida Water

  Olive oil

  Basin to catch your cleansing bathwater (if taking a
      shower)

  1 cup sea salt

  3 drops eucalyptus essential oil

  3 drops rosemary essential oil

  Container to carry your bathwater to the crossroads

Clean clothes

Smoky quartz

A small piece of lightning-struck wood (available online
where fine Hoodoo products are sold or from a place
where lightning has struck a tree)

1 square of camphor

Timing

Crossroads hour—midnight.

Waning cycle of the moon—this period occurs after a
full moon. It lasts until the new moon. You can easily see this
period by checking a calendar. This time of the moon cycle is
good for letting go of things that no longer serve you. This is
exactly what we are seeking to accomplish. We are seeking to
let go of haunting feelings, disturbing thoughts, and distractions that do not serve us.

Crossroads Preparation: A Cleansing Bath

Cleanse the tealights with Florida Water and anoint them with
olive oil. Light the tealights and set them outside your bath so
you can step between them after bathing.

Run a bath or shower. Turn on the water and set it to a
comfortable temperature. If you're taking a shower, place your
basin at the bottom of the shower so you can capture the water.

Before you step into your bath, fill your container with
warm water. Add the sea salt and the eucalyptus and rosemary
essential oils to the water.

Step into your bath with your container of salted, scented water. Be careful. Don't get any in your eyes. You're already blind with rage and emotion, and you need to see!

As you hold your container filled with water, sea salt, and rosemary and eucalyptus essential oils, close your eyes; take a deep breath. Inhale the cleansing aromas from the salted mixture you have created. Take a moment to relax and go deeply into yourself.

Lift the container of water and pour the water over yourself. As you pour the water over your body, visualize the wings of Lilith lifting you above your troubles, giving you the strength to set yourself free from the worries and troubles that disturb your sleep, plague your serenity, and intrude upon your waking thoughts.

When your container of cleansing water is empty, scoop some of the water from the tub or basin into your container.

Step from your bath between the lit tealights, carrying the container filled with your bathwater. Set your container down and pinch out the tealights. You can save the tealights for when you do this ritual again, or you can use them in the sacred space you'll create for the Goddess Lilith.

Prepare yourself to go to the crossroads.

Put on clean clothes. Gather your container of bathwater.

Place the smoky quartz, lightning-struck wood, and camphor square in your pocket.

At the Crossroads

Step into the crossroads at midnight. Face west. Take the square of camphor from your pocket and sprinkle it on the ground. Throw your bathwater over your left shoulder.

Take the lightning-struck wood and smoky quartz from your pocket. Hold them in your hand. Kiss them. Say a prayer over them for strength, power, and protection.

Thank the Goddess Lilith for cleansing your dreams; strengthening your mind, body, and spirit; and helping you with your plight. Step out of the crossroads and don't look back. Not looking back is your statement of faith. Now is the time to believe in the work you have done.

Go home by a different route. Place the lightning-struck wood and smoky quartz on your altar or sleep with them under your pillow for a few nights.

Go to bed and wake up to a new morning light.

* * *

Creating a Sacred Space for Lilith

After you have completed your ritual for the Goddess Lilith, you may want to connect with her on a regular basis, outside of the ritual described. Creating a sacred altar space for the goddess you have called upon to aid you is a lovely, magickal way to keep her powerful presence in your life. You can leave the altar up for as long as you deem necessary. You can also create

this sacred space without performing the ritual described; however, you will find the sacred space more meaningful once you
have the called upon the goddess to aid you in your troubles.

Items Needed

Lilith statue (available online from metaphysical stores or
   spiritual supply shops)

Lightning-struck wood

Smoky quartz

Moonstone (a stone of protection that symbolizes the
   Divine Feminine)

Cloves *(Eugenia caryophyllata)*, a small handful

Mugwort *(Artemisia vulgaris)*, a small handful

Tarot card VIII: Strength

Feathers (symbolizing Lilith's powerful wings)

Black cloth to cover the surface area designated as Lilith's
   sacred space

These nine items symbolize the ability, the power to endure,
and the strength to overcome. Place them in a space where,
upon passing them, your courage soars, your confidence is
stoked, and you remember your badass self who went to the
crossroads at midnight to effect positive change in your life. If
it isn't safe to display these items, store them in a box or a container and keep them in a secret spot known only to you.

To create your sacred space, arrange the items around the
Lilith statue. It matters not how you place your items; just
allow the Lilith statue to be the center of the display.

During the waning moon cycle, light a candle upon your altar and reflect upon the magick and strength you received during your Lilith ritual at the crossroads. Listen to Annie Lennox sing "Missionary Man," and let that music encourage you. You can also pause and reflect at your sacred space dedicated to Lilith anytime you feel called to invoke the power of this goddess.

three
OVERCOMING PAIN
WITH FRIDA KAHLO

Song: **"Keep Looking"**
Artist: **Sade**

FRIDA KAHLO WAS BORN on July 6, 1907, in Coyoacán, Mexico City, Mexico. Frida Kahlo's life has been the subject of art exhibits, films, movies, paintings, and countless expressions in her honor. We know through books, film, and art that she suffered tremendously. She survived horrific surgeries and the methods of medical science of her time to ease her pain. In the end, she died with her eyes open, hoping never to return. She passed away on July 13, 1954, in Coyoacán, Mexico City, Mexico.

Frida Kahlo was a legendary painter and artist and is considered a contemporary feminist icon. She not only stands the test of time through her immortal

39

paintings and art, but she also looks straight into our souls through countless black-and-white photos taken of her during her lifetime. One of my favorite photos shows her sitting in a straight-backed chair, holding a cigarette. In this self-portrait, her gaze is intimidating and alluring (Castello-Cortes 2018, 61). According to the text accompanying the photo, it was taken shortly after she had a miscarriage, and it wasn't her first loss of a child.

How sad!

Yet here she sits, strong and composed, gazing directly into the camera, telling us she isn't done yet. We know her body betrayed her many times. Yet in this photo she shows strength, courage, and resilience. She defies pity. She suffered through so many physical traumas and ordeals, sadness and grief, yet she became someone who exemplified the willingness and ability to carry on in the darkest of times. She truly left her mark upon the world.

Her marriage to the world-famous painter Diego Rivera was well documented. Not only did Frida endure pain from her body, but she also suffered through a tumultuous marriage. She stated she suffered two grave accidents her life: "One ... a streetcar ... the other ... Diego" (Castello-Cortes 2018, 40).

Frida Kahlo was a mortal being. She is someone we can relate to, as a person who experienced these deep, dark, and troubling times. Call upon her to help you go the distance. She is no saint, but she is deserving of the title "goddess." I see her as a goddess of pain and suffering, a symbol of triumph and overcoming.

Through looking at and appreciating the life of Frida Kahlo, we ascend the mountain of struggle, of trying to express ourselves uniquely, to make a mark in the world, while suffering tremendous heartache and burdens.

Frida Kahlo is the goddess for all artists and creatives. She is the patroness of holding your head up high. She is the beacon of *don't quit*, even when your body and the world are against you. In the end, you will triumph, and all those who doubted you will be the first to bring you flowers.

Soul Speak

I came face-to-face with the art of Frida Kahlo in an exhibit at the Philadelphia Museum of Art in 2008. Long had I admired her. Long had she soothed my heart. Together, a fellow admirer and I climbed the tall steps to the museum, the same steps made famous in the blockbuster movie *Rocky* starring Sylvester Stallone.

When we reached the top of the stairs and entered the museum, we came face-to-face with a monumental statue of the Goddess Diana. She was resplendent and powerful in her stance, her bronze strength emanating through her stature, as she pulled back her bow, ready to shoot her arrow at her target. The spell was cast.

When we entered the Frida Kahlo exhibit, a hush fell over the admirers. Everyone quietly waited their turn to view her work. You could hear people gasp as their eyes gazed upon Frida Kahlo's paintings and photographs, which displayed the depth and agony of her soul. Some pieces you admired; others made you clutch your breath. So vivid and heart wrenching they were, you could only look, not speak.

She wore pants in some photos. In others, she wore roses in her hair and smoked a cigarette. And always, her beautiful eyebrows that grew together were prominent.

Frida Kahlo cannot be explained. She can only be felt, experienced.

I feel her through the myriad candles dedicated to her, which people can now easily purchase. I experience her through the tiny altar kit I purchased at the art exhibit in Philadelphia. I feel her through the undeniably splendid portrayal of her life in the movie *Frida* by iconic actress Salma Hayek.

The legacy of Frida Kahlo is one we can turn to when we are experiencing a dark night of the soul. A dark night of the soul is when you feel emotionally and spiritually abandoned. It can be a time of deep questioning and losing faith. Yet it can also lead to inspiration, creativity, and freedom of expression.

"Keep Looking" ~ Why I Chose This Song for Goddess Frida Kahlo

In the song "Keep Looking," Sade bids us to keep going. She persuades us not to focus on our problems. She urges us not to listen to naysayers—those who don't understand or appreciate us, especially those who bash us and are unsupportive. She inspires us to turn a blind eye to those who seek to undermine our creativity or expression with self-inflated senses of superiority or authority.

When we think upon the ideals of courage, strength, deter-mination, and perseverance, the struggle against insurmount-able odds, the great Frida Kahlo stands high upon the moun-taintop as a beacon for feelings of not being understood or appreciated.

●●●●●●●●●●●●●●●●●●●

Triumph Over Pain and Suffering Ritual

In *Desperately Seeking Frida* by Ian Castello-Cortes, the author states, "Frida Kahlo, her eyes open in a fixed stare, had died quietly alone, in the night" (page 136).

Oh, my heart. After everything she had been through—all her suffering, achievements, and accomplishments—she had passed over, died, with her eyes wide open, staring.

She was looking up.

She died with her eyes open, looking ahead, hopefully into the afterlife she so continuously longed for.

Many of us long for a release, especially when the burden is heavy or we feel misunderstood or poignantly misjudged, crippled by self-doubt or, worse, self-loathing. I know. I've been there many times. Yet, underneath that devastating self-doubt or imposter syndrome, I've always known my visions, goals, and dreams are real and important and that they matter.

Perhaps you, too, have felt that way. When your back is against the wall and you're doubting all you've set forth to achieve—when you can't see your way and the world seems dark, like it's telling you to let go of this foolishness—the triumphant life of Frida Kahlo and the deep, strong voice of Sade tell us to keep looking and carry on.

Pain. Frida was in pain. Real pain. Crippling pain. Physical pain. A lot of what I am writing about in this book speaks to ways of coping through spiritual or emotional pain. One of the things that makes Goddess Frida Kahlo so different is she suffered through tremendous physical pain while she also created works of incredible, gut-wrenching, soul-blinding art.

Perhaps that is why I feel her so and seek to honor her as I write these words. During the time I was writing this book, I, too, was in pain. Real pain. And this pain gives me a different perspective—a minute lens into what it is like to try to create when your body is not cooperating and the pain is real.

See, I fell.

I tripped over my goddamn shoe. I tripped over it, and I went down hard, on my knee.

Excruciating pain. I thought I'd broken something in my kneecap. The physicians who first saw me thought so, too. They diagnosed me with a fractured patella. But images taken later showed I had a bone contusion and immense swelling on my knee.

Crutches. Ice. Medication. Rest. Anger. Frustration. Am I grateful I didn't need surgery? Of course I am. Am I frustrated with being in pain every day since my injury occurred? Yes.

At the time of this writing, I still can't bend my left knee. I can't reach the bottom of my foot. I try to get around without my crutch for periods, and then I just have to give in, grab my crutch, use it to walk, or sit down, and elevate my leg. Rest. Ice.

I can only imagine how Frida Kahlo felt when her physical pain would take hold of her.

When you're in pain, you want it to stop. And you mourn the loss of your body when it was normal, and you could just do what you wanted to do.

My injury will hopefully heal and, hopefully, by the time you read these words, my knee will have returned to normal. I can only pray that it will.* For Frida, we know her injuries continued to worsen, and her health spiraled downward, until the release of death set her free.

So those of us who love her, those of us who have also suffered with real physical pain, appreciate the rawness of her art. We appreciate what it must have taken for her to continue to create, dress herself so wonderfully, and carry on. We appreciate what it must have taken for her to keep her artistic visions alive when she was faced with insurmountable odds. Those of us who are creatives know the struggle of trying to birth our visions into the world. We know what it takes to call forth and manifest a vision, a creative idea. We understand the struggle, the striving and determination, to see our ideas become a tangible form—one we can hold, touch, read, or listen to. We see you, Goddess Frida Kahlo. We deeply respect your suffering and your pain and what you accomplished as a human being while you were alive on this earth plane.

So, when the pain of life—be it physical, emotional, or spiritual—comes at you, like the swords of nightmares stabbing you, robbing you of your precious sleep and serenity, robbing you of peace, like the figure on the tarot card Nine of Swords or a visceral, gut-wrenching painting by Frida Kahlo, this is the time to perform this rite, to triumph over pain and suffering. Play Sade's "Keep Looking," listen to her soothing words, and allow her harmonic waves to wash over you as you gather your items for your ritual and enter into sacred space to open your heart and mind to spiritual healing.

★My knee healed, and I'm now getting around just fine!

Items Needed

Altar cloth, black

Tarot card: Nine of Swords

Image of Frida Kahlo

Ceramic or printed images of doves

Tiny skulls

Red roses

Vase

Fireproof container

Charcoal disk

A small piece of dragon's blood resin

Timing

Dusk, twilight hour.

Preparation

Cover your altar with the black altar cloth. Place the Nine of Swords tarot card, the image of Frida Kahlo, and the ceramic or printed images of doves on the altar. Arrange the tiny skulls in a circle around the tarot card, the image of Frida Kahlo, and the doves. Place the red roses in a vase on the altar.

In a fireproof container, light the charcoal disk. Once the disk is hot, place the dragon's blood resin on the charcoal. As the smoke rises from the charcoal, say,

> Oh Frida, I know you have long since gone away.
> It was your wish and desire not to stay.
> You suffered, you triumphed. You shed light and brought
> mercy to your own plight. I, too, Frida, am suffering.
> Help me overcome and triumph. Show me the way out
> and through. Help me, Frida. With love in my heart, I
> offer this prayer for guidance and protection unto you.

Allow the dragon's blood resin to burn out completely. Carry the roses to a cemetery and leave them at the gate. Go home a different way than the way you came. Know your rite is over, your ritual is done.

Creating a Sacred Space for Frida Kahlo

After you have completed your ritual for Goddess Frida Kahlo, you may want to connect with her on a regular basis, outside of the ritual described. Creating a sacred altar space for the goddess you have called upon to aid you is a lovely, magickal way to keep her powerful presence in your life. You can leave the altar up for as long as you deem necessary. You can also create this sacred space without performing the ritual described; however, you will find the sacred space more meaningful once you have the called upon the goddess to aid you in your troubles.

Items Needed

Image of Frida Kahlo

Flower vase

Flowers, fresh or faux (just cleanse them with Florida Water)

Faux fruit

A small, pretty bottle of perfume

Makeup: blush, powder, mascara

Ribbons

Mexican sweets or candies

To create a sacred space for Frida Kahlo, any flat surface will do. You can use the top of a dresser, a cubby, or a shelf in a closet. Just be sure to clean the space and bless it with Florida Water.

Arrange the items listed in a pleasing fashion. Frida loved fresh fruit, but for your altar, use faux fruit that is easily found in craft stores. Frida loved to dress well, she was an expert at applying her makeup, and she loved the expensive perfume Schiaparelli. For your altar purposes, inexpensive makeup that is easily found at stores can pay homage to the beauty of Frida Kahlo, and a perfume in a pretty bottle that calls to you will do as a replacement for the expensive Schiaparelli.

Frida also loved Mexican sweets and candies. These may be harder to find if you don't live in an area that has these cultural items. If you can find them, add them to your sacred space. If not, you can use some nice sweets that you find pleasing.

Once you have all your items, set them up on the space you've designated for Frida. Personally, I have a small altar purchased from the gift shop at the Philadelphia Museum of Art, where I attended her exhibit in 2008. This premade altar gift package was a bag filled with all types of goodies: pieces of blue wood, feathers, bottle caps, tiny toys, and a small portrait of Frida. I had a lot of fun putting this small home altar together.

I placed the altar where I can see Frida Kahlo's face on a daily basis, and after doing research for this chapter, I've also added some of the items listed above. I also have Frida Kahlo candles and a little table decorated with images of Frida that I purchased at a Hispanic celebration and craft fair. I'm always on the lookout for things that call me to Frida Kahlo.

May your sacred space in honor of her bring you strength, love, courage, and joy.

In *Desperately Seeking Frida*, author Ian Castello-Cortes lists several museums and galleries that have exhibited Frida's work. He states, "Adherents of her work queue for hours patiently to feel Frida's emotions, to experience Frida's magic" (140).

When we seek to create a sacred space for Frida Kahlo, we do so from a place of homage, acknowledgment, and respect. We seek only to honor and remember her as an incredible woman, artist, and human being who lived an extraordinary, incredible life.

four

calling marie laveau for comfort for court cases

Song: "Willow"
Artist: Joan Armatrading

THE NEXT TWO CHAPTERS focus on rites working with the divine Goddesses Marie Laveau and Manman Brijit for assistance with court case work. They are lengthy chapters that require time and study before performing the rites. Some of the instructions may seem out of your comfort zone. That's okay. When you or a loved one is facing the judge, jail, or a jury, *you are out of your comfort zone.* There is nothing cozy or welcoming about the situation. So please bear that in mind as you step into court case works with Marie Laveau and Manman Brijit.

Marie Laveau was born September 10, 1801, in New Orleans, Louisiana. She is admired and honored as a goddess, a Lwa (a Vodou deity), in New Orleans Vodou. She was a Master Hoodoo Practitioner and an icon of courage, strength, and protection. She can be called upon to assist in triumphing over court cases, and in these modern times, she is seen as a contemporary feminist icon and a legendary magickal Woman of Color.

Marie Laveau was a magnificent Woman of Color who lived in the 1800s in New Orleans, Louisiana. She had a commanding presence and gave of herself and her time to help others in need. She made herself available to people who had few avenues of assistance to turn to when they were in trouble.

She passed from her human life on June 16, 1881, in New Orleans, Louisiana. So beloved was Marie Laveau that when she passed over, her obituary was printed in the *Times-Picayune* newspaper, which was quite a testament to a Woman of Color who lived in New Orleans during the 1800s. To this day, people still flock to her tomb to pay their respects and leave offerings.

Soul Speak

While many people associate the Divine Marie Laveau with snakes, oils, charms, and gris-gris bags, what is less often talked about is the work she did in her community, the work she did for those suffering and languishing in prison. Mama Marie (as I affectionately call her) was routinely known to visit the sick and infirmed. Her visit to Cabildo prison to bring spiritual alleviation to those under the thumb of the law is well documented.

In her book *A New Orleans Vodou Priestess: The Legend and Reality of Marie of Laveau*, author Carolyn Morrow Long states, "The Picayune obituary went on to describe Marie's many admirable traits ... Marie, it was noted, 'labored incessantly,' to comfort condemned prisoners, praying with them in their last moments and endeavoring to rescue them from the gallows" (Morrow Long 2006, XXIV).

Author Lyle Saxon in his book *Fabulous New Orleans* recounts a story of Marie Laveau, which appeared in an article by G. William Nott, which appeared in the *Times-Picayune*:

> "It will not be amiss to relate the story of an octo-
> genarian mammy, who says that Marie Laveau
> was not a wicked woman, but much maligned by
> her enemies, and that what powers she had were
> used for the good of others as the following tale
> will prove. A certain wealthy young man in New
> Orleans, many years ago, had been arrested in
> connection with a crime, and though his compan-
> ions were in reality the guilty ones, the blame was
> laid upon his shoulders. The grief-stricken father
> immediately sought Marie Laveau, explained to
> her the circumstances of the case, and offered her
> a handsome reward if she would obtain his son's
> release.
>
> "When the day set for the trial came round,
> the wily 'voodoo,' after placing three Guinea pep-
> pers in her mouth, entered the St. Louis Cathe-
> dral, knelt at the altar rail, and was seen to remain

in this posture for some time. Leaving the church, she gained admittance to the Cabildo, where the trial was to be held, and depositing three of the peppers under the judge's bench, lingered to await developments.

"After a lengthy deliberation, though the evidence seemed unfavorable to the prisoner, the jury finally made its report, and the judge was heard to pronounce the words, 'Not Guilty.' The joy of the anxious father may well be imagined. His first act was to find Marie Laveau and, as a recompense for her miraculous intervention, he gave her the deed to a small cottage. The latter, situated on St. Anne between Rampart and Burgundy, remained her home to the time of her death"

(Saxon 1928, 244).

Yes indeed! Now we know how Marie Laveau came to live in her famous cottage, located in the French Quarter of New Orleans.

Sallie Ann Glassman in her book *Vodou Visions* states, "During her [Marie Laveau's] life, she was known to be exceptionally kind and caring to the poor, to prisoners, and to victims of yellow fever" (Glassman 2007, 53).

A note about the text quoted from Lyle Saxon's book and its use of the word *mammy*. I don't like it. It's not a word I use, nor do I appreciate its usage referring to elder Women of

Color. However, Lyle Saxon's book was published in 1928, and he, too, is quoting from an older source. In keeping true to the text, as it was written, I kept the word, but that doesn't mean I didn't wince when I read it.

Marie Laveau is deserving of our love and respect. While many seek her as a Vodou Queen for assistance in their magickal endeavors, beyond that, she is deserving of recognition and honor for a life well lived in service to her community and those in need. As she continues to call to us from beyond the veil of Spirit, let us remember her for the extraordinary life she lived.

"Willow" ~ Why I Chose This Song for Goddess Marie Laveau

As I write these words about Marie Laveau, the sun is setting on this day in November. I've listened to the song "Willow" by Joan Armatrading so many times I've lost count. Joan's words and music entered my life way back in the 1980s, when I worked in a record store in Boulder, Colorado. "Willow" soothed my soul then, and now it calls to me as a song for the Divine Marie Laveau. I weep every time I listen to it.

A willow tree. A gigantic willow tree used to stand in the center in one of my favorite places, the Denver Botanic Gardens. For years I would make my way to the Denver Botanic Gardens, my sanctuary in the city. I'd take my time and wander through the gardens, the paths, making my way to the enormous willow tree, whose branches almost touched the water, in the pond, in the Japanese garden. I was heartbroken when this beloved tree had to be removed due to fungus. Its spirit still lives in the place it used to stand. And I remember it every time I visit the Gardens.

I love willow trees. One only need gaze upon their long, weeping branches to understand why they bring such comfort. They give shade when the sun is too hot, and their bark is a favorite wand of Witches.

In the song "Willow," Joan Armatrading's voice gives us shelter in a storm. Joan was a comfort to me. I used to love looking at her album covers. I loved her big afro, and her strong features. Her lyrics and music came into my life at a tender time. Joan Armatrading was and still is an icon of a powerful, visionary Black Woman. She remains a legend in her own time.

And, oh, Mama Marie. She is a shelter and a comfort for us. Although she is so often misunderstood, she waits patiently, fervently, for us to acknowledge her with love, respect, grace.

I remember the first time I made my way to her tomb. This was before the cemetery was shut to visitors wishing to visit the tomb of Marie Laveau. Due to an act of vandalism, one can now only visit her tomb with a tour guide.

I was so nervous. I remember entering the cemetery by myself. A cemetery attendant asked me if I needed help. I could have told the attendant I was looking for the tomb of Marie Laveau, but in my heart, I knew I needed to find her tomb by myself. It was part of my journey. In my mind, if I had to get directions to find her tomb, then I wasn't worthy of leaving an offering and asking for her help. If it was meant to be, I'd find it.

And find it I did. There was a group in front of her tomb with a guide. I waited patiently for the group to leave so I could be alone in front of the white walls of her tomb covered with Xs and offerings left on the ground.

As I approached the tomb, a Black Man, a caregiver for the cemetery, seemed to appear out of nowhere. We talked for a moment. I told him I was there to leave my offerings for Marie Laveau, but I was nervous. He told me to do what I needed to do. Before I left my offerings, I helped him clean up the area in front of Marie Laveau's tomb. And when I was finished, he gifted me with a precious memento that I've kept with me all these years. It was truly a life-changing, magickal experience.

The Divine Marie Laveau continues to accept the countless offerings and prayers left at her tomb and her shrine, located in the New Orleans Healing Center. And contrary to what many would have us believe, her power continues to grow and draw people to her, over one hundred thirty years after her physical body was laid to rest.

Rite for Spiritual Guidance and Assistance with Court Cases from Marie Laveau

This rite is for appearances in court. Depending on the nature of the court case, the case may be resolved in one day, or it could continue for an unspecified amount of time. The wheels of justice turn slowly.

Items Needed

Glass Novena/seven-day brown candle

Court case oil (available at metaphysical supply stores and spiritual botanicas)

Blessing oil (available at metaphysical supply stores and spiritual botanicas)

John the Conqueror root oil (available at metaphysical supply stores and spiritual botanicas)

Florida Water

Pushpin or nail

Brown permanent marker

Altar cloth, blue and white

Image of Marie Laveau

Small chime 4-inch or birthday-size blue candle

Candle holder for small chime 4-inch or birthday-size blue candle

Small chime 4-inch or birthday-size white candle

Candle holder for small chime 4-inch or birthday-size white candle

Flowers, blue and white

Salt

Water

Small container to hold salted water

Little John to Chew root (available at metaphysical supply stores and spiritual botanicas)

Sugar water (add a few teaspoons of sugar to a half cup of water)

Timing
Whenever you need to do this work.

Preparation
Dress and fix the glass Novena/seven-day brown candle with court case oil, blessing oil, and John the Conqueror root oil.

To Dress and Fix the Candle
Pour a small amount of Florida Water on top of the brown wax in the candle. Swirl the Florida Water around the inside of the glass. Dip your finger into the Florida Water on the wax and wipe the rim of the glass candle. Next, anoint your finger with Florida Water from the candle, and on the outside of the candle, starting at the middle, wipe upward to the rim. Then wipe downward to the bottom of the candle.

Next, using a pushpin or a nail, poke seven holes in a circular pattern into the candle wax. Pour out any extra Florida Water. Add three drops each of the court case oil, blessing oil, and John the Conqueror root oil. Remember, when adding oils to candles, less is more. Adding too much oil can cause the wick to not burn properly. Once you've added the oils, swirl them around the wax.

On the outer glass of the candle, write the court attendee's name using the brown marker. Also write the words *freedom* and *victory*. Once you are finished writing, make a fist. Using your fist, knock three times on the side of the candle. Then tap the candle three times on the table. As you knock and tap the candle, say,

This candle is dressed and fixed for [insert name]. May
they be abundantly blessed and protected through all
their trials and tribulations. May the best and highest
outcome manifest for them in accordance with their
highest good. Blessed be. So mote it be.

Set the candle aside.

For the Rite

Upon your altar, place the blue and white altar cloths and the image of Marie Laveau. Cleanse your blue and white candles with Florida Water.

Place the blue candle in its candle holder, next to Marie Laveau's image, and the white candle in its candle holder, on the other side of her image.

Lay the blue and white flowers in front of Marie's image.

Place your dressed and fixed brown candle in front of Marie Laveau's image.

Gather your salt and water and the small container to hold the salted water.

Say,

Blessed is this salt.
Blessed is this water.

Pour the water into the container.
Sprinkle three pinches of salt into the water.
Light the blue and white candles.

Holding the salted water in your hands (the salted water represents your tears, for surely court cases wrench and tear at your heart), stand in place, turn clockwise, then counterclockwise, then clockwise again.

Place the salted water on the altar.

Light the brown candle.

Call upon Marie Laveau with humility and sincerity.

From your heart, speak your troubles unto Marie. Tell her of your woes and fears. Say a sincere and heartfelt prayer for yourself or your loved one who is experiencing the trials and tribulations of court. Ask her and thank her for watching over and protecting you or your loved one.

When you have finished your prayers, pinch out the blue and white candles. Allow the salted water to evaporate. Allow the brown candle to burn until you know the outcome of that day's court appearance.

Note: If you are uncomfortable leaving the brown candle burning while you are away, snuff out the candle and allow it to sit upon your altar for Marie Laveau until you know the outcome of the court appearance.

Remember, we only snuff out candles we use in spiritual workings if we can't allow them to safely burn out. Pinching or snuffing out the flame is a spiritual message the work is ongoing. Blowing out a flame means the work is done.

Once you know the outcome of the court appearance, will there be another appearance, or has the situation been resolved? You can either leave the altar for Marie up (if it is safe to do so), or you can store all the altar pieces and the seven-day candle in a safe place until the next court appearance.

If the situation has been resolved and the brown candle did not burn all the way down, keep lighting the candle daily until the flame burns out on its own. This way, you will bring the spell to a successful close.

Prior to Court Appearance Day, to Assist the Person Going to Court

Soak the Little John to Chew root in sugar water overnight. Give it to the person before their day in court. Instruct the person to chew the root and spit the juices onto their palms before they enter the courthouse. Tell them not to touch anyone after they spit the root juice onto their palms.

Instruct them to touch the doors of the courthouse, go through the metal detectors, and so on with the Little John to Chew juice on their palms. If possible, instruct them to also touch the chairs or pews of the courtroom. Sometimes a person will need to use the restroom before they enter the courtroom. Once they've washed their hands, it's okay for them to touch other people.

If spitting on your hands makes you or the person you are working for uncomfortable, feel free to omit this step. As always, one must follow their gut instincts when performing spell work of any kind. *However,* in the spirit of this type of powerful juju, spitting the root juice on one's hands is a powerful act of sympathetic magick, which can boost the confidence of the person going to court.

Note: Court cases are long and involved. Rarely does a court case end in just one appearance before the judge, unless the matter is a traffic or one-day incident. Be prepared to do this work of lighting the candle, petitioning Marie Laveau, and performing the above rite *every time* your loved one has a court appearance.

In my experience, it is best to light the candle the night before the court date, then allow the candle to burn in a safe, fireproof container while the person is in court. If the issue is resolved in court that day, allow the candle to burn completely out and recycle the glass container. If there is another court date set (which is highly probable) after each court appearance, snuff out the candle and save it for the next court date.

In working court cases, we can never be sure of the outcome. But we do our best to work with Spirit, Marie Laveau, and our ancestors to ensure the best possible outcome for the person who stands before the judge.

And, if possible, once the case has been successfully resolved, make your way to New Orleans to thank Marie Laveau.

A word about how a "successful" outcome may be interpreted. A dismissal of charges may not happen. However, lesser or no jail time, work release, probation or supervised probation, no fees or fines, or not having to come back to court over and over again are all variations of a successful outcome.

If a person is facing time, just going to court and exiting the front door is a good day! Not having your loved one hauled off to jail through the back door in the courtroom is a good day! The courtroom is a tricky, scary, and volatile place.

So, try to remain open-minded as to what a successful outcome may be, and let Marie Laveau, your ancestors, and your Higher Power and Spirit work for you.

* * * * * * * * * * * * * * * * * *

Creating a Sacred Space for Marie Laveau

After you have completed your ritual for the Divine Marie Laveau, you may want to connect with her on a regular basis, outside of the ritual described. Creating a sacred altar space for the goddess you have called upon to aid you is a lovely, magickal way to keep her powerful presence in your life. You can leave the altar up for as long as you deem necessary. You can also create this sacred space without performing the ritual described; however, you will find the sacred space more meaningful once you have called upon the goddess to aid you in your troubles.

Items Needed

Florida Water

A statue or candle bearing the likeness of Marie Laveau*
   *Please note that a true portrait of Marie Laveau was never painted. Connect with an image that speaks to you.

A blue candle

A white candle

A white cloth

A seashell

A bowl of water

A small amount of salt

Fireproof candleholders

The legacy and life of Marie Laveau are steeped in mystery. What little factual knowledge we know about her has already been written. What remains is what we bring to her from our love, honor, and respect.

I came to Marie because she was and is an iconic Woman of Color, of power and magick.

Long had I toiled in the soil of the Craft seeking to align with a deity, a goddess, a myth or legend who looked like me, an African American, Black Woman of Color. Meaning no disrespect to the Orishas or deities of the African Diasporic Religions, what drew me to Marie Laveau was that she was a living person and an African American. I could relate to her. I could see myself in her. I could actually go to her tomb and make offerings to her. I could retrace her steps and her life in my mind, and through my initiation into Vodou, I could connect with her in much deeper ways.

As we set about to create a sacred space for Marie Laveau, let us bring her into these modern times. I will share how I connect in sacred space with her, but I also encourage you to allow her spirit and guidance to show you the way. Her spirit is still close to us, having only passed from human life little more than a hundred years ago.

When you seek to create her sacred space, do so from a place of respect. Look to her as you would a beloved elder, grandmother, or wise old friend. She is deserving of nothing less and so much more.

When you speak of her, hold her name in reverence and gently educate those who may only know a Hollywood version of her. Remind people of her strength, power, and grace.

Remind people how she cared for the sick, the poor, and the infirmed. How she often visited and comforted those in prison.

If possible, the sacred space you create for Marie Laveau should remain up and visible to you once you have created it. If it is not safe for this space to remain up, please find the nicest box or container you can to store all your items.

Once you have gathered all your items, cleanse them with Florida Water: Cleanse the statue or candle. Cleanse your blue and white candles. Anoint your white cloth.

Lay out your white cloth. Upon it, place your image of Marie Laveau. In front of her image, place your seashell, bowl of water, and salt. On either side of her candle or statue, place the blue and white candles in their candleholders.

I have incorporated lighting my candles to Marie Laveau during the time of the full moon; however, you can perform the lighting of your candles whenever you feel called to connect with her.

You can also connect to her during the Summer Solstice or on St. John's Eve. Both holidays normally fall on or around June 21. The St. John's Eve ceremonies Marie Laveau held on Bayou St. John in New Orleans are famous historical moments. Thousands of people would line the banks to see her rise from the waters of the Bayou (Morrow Long 2006, 6).

Next, pour a small amount of water into your seashell. Sprinkle three pinches of salt into the water.

Light your candles.

Holding your seashell of salted water, turn clockwise, then counterclockwise, then clockwise. Offer your salted water to Marie Laveau. Place your shell of salted water upon your sacred space. Thank her for guidance, blessings, and protection.

Once you have finished connecting with Marie Laveau in your sacred space, if your candles are still burning, pinch them or snuff them out. Save them for the next time you connect in this sacred space.

Allow the salted water to evaporate, letting the air carry it forth.

Continue your practice of connecting with Marie Laveau on a consistent basis. As you put in the time and effort, your relationship to and with her will continue to grow and blossom. If you feel called to go deeper into Vodou, spend time in the sacred space you created for Marie Laveau. Share with her your desire to go further and deeper and allow her to be your guide.

five
seekiNG iNterveNtioN iN court cases from maNmaN brijit

Song: "Other Side of the Game"
Artist: Erykah Badu

IF YOU OR YOUR loved one is facing the strong arm of the law, the heavy bang of the gavel, consider engaging with this next level of deep juju for troubled times. You can go to the graveyard and place your petition to Manman Brijit (this is *not* the Goddess Brigid of Celtic origin, for whom we light candles during the Sabbat of Imbolc), tell her of your troubles, and ask for her help.

According to Sallie Ann Glassman, Manbo and author of *Vodou Visons*, "Manman Brijit is considered to be a supreme judge and lawyer" (Glassman 2007,

113). Manman Brijit is a Lwa—a Vodou deity—who is considered a goddess, the Protectress of the Cemetery. She is the wife of Baron Samedi, who is also a Lwa. She is associated with the first woman buried in a cemetery. Manman Brijit and Baron Samedi belong to the Ghede family of Vodou. The Ghede are the Lwa of the dead and the cemetery.

As a mother in the Spirit World, Manman Brijit understands the pain of loss and the fear of losing someone you love to an unjust system or situation. Her arms reach out to us from beyond the crossroads, as we reach to her. Yes, it can be a daunting experience to call upon her, but when you or your loved ones are facing the possibility of jail time, the courage to show up and do what you need to do rises to the top of your being. You are able to go the distance with the help of Manman Brijit and be there, strong—for yourself, or for your loved ones.

Soul Speak

When you or someone you love is facing *time*, things get nasty. Sometimes situations with the court won't resolve easily or end. When we or our loved ones are facing serious consequences with the US court system, it's a nightmare from which you pray to awake at the earliest dawn.

It is not my place to judge the situation you or your loved one may be facing. I can only say this from personal experience: when someone you love is facing the loss of their freedom, looking at potentially serious jail time or being locked up behind bars, as a magickal and spiritual person, you will do whatever you can to help them.

And don't get me started on the grief and anguish mothers of Black sons face. There are too many young Black Men locked up in prison. That's why we have "the talk" with our kids. We know the system wants them. And we will call upon whomever and whatever to keep our babies out of jail.

Only our humanity will save us. One cannot look upon human beings in shackles and chains without their compassion welling up, no matter the reason for those shackles. I know this because I have seen it, witnessed it. It didn't matter the person's skin color, ethnicity, gender, or race. I have had the occasion to sit in a courtroom and look upon fellow human beings chained up. It didn't matter to me what the charges were or if they were justified; I just know seeing a human being in a jumpsuit and shackles tears at my heart in deep places. We know there are crimes that deserve punishment. I'm just talking about seeing another human being shackled and chained.

A word of caution: before you make this petition, you must be absolutely truthful, honest, and sincere with yourself. I suggest you take some time to meditate and pray and ask for guidance. We don't tell lies to Manman Brijit. And we certainly don't want to make promises we cannot keep.

If you take it upon yourself to do this work for another person, have a frank talk with them about the charges they are facing and their part in the situation. Ask them to tell you the truth about what happened, for if you do this work for them, you, too, are entering into an agreement with Manman Brijit, and you must be sure and clear once you undertake the work.

"Other Side of the Game" ~ Why I Chose
This Song for Goddess Manman Brijit

The songstress and poetess Erykah Badu "keeps it real," as folks like me like to say. When you listen to her song "Other Side of the Game," you know things have gotten deep. Just by hearing the words and feeling the power of Erykah Badu's voice, our soul and spirit connect with the chilling fear of the strong arm of the law. We know what she is talking about. And we know who "they" are.

Someone or something bad is coming for her love. The shadow is no longer hovering, it's coming. What we're talking about here is time … *time*. The time of you or a loved one doing *time*. Don't know what that means? Then perhaps this rite and chapter aren't for you. If you know what I'm talking about, read on.

For the previous rite, we worked with the Divine Marie Laveau. That rite was for when you're caught going to court day after day for months or even years. But for many, there comes a moment when the system changes and sends out its cold, icy fingers for your or your loved one's freedom. It stalks your peace and mind and serenity. The *fear* is real, and you know it.

You know the possibility of it winning. You know it's reaching for you or your loved one. You know it wants to put them behind bars. And the system getting another "win" is a real, valid, tangible possibility. And that possibility scares the hell out of you. I'm just going to tell you like it is. No matter how TV or movies or songs glorify jail or prison, nobody in their right mind wants to go to prison or see their loved one behind bars.

Manman Brijit is the goddess, the Lwa, we turn to when things have gotten deep and real. Manman Brijit waits patiently for us in the cemetery. From her image printed on a candle, given to me at my New Orleans Vodou Society's Fet Ghede ceremony, she sits cross-legged atop a pile of stones in the grave-yard. Her eyes are plugged with cotton. She holds a lit candle, while other lit candles grace her shrine of stones. A hand offers a lit candle to her. She waits for our plea, our entreaty. She's seen so many things and has helped so many. She can help you, too, if you call upon her correctly, with reverence and respect.

Manman Brijit Cemetery Rite for Inspirational Intervention for Court Cases

For this rite, you will be working with the oldest woman bur-ied in the cemetery. Some cemeteries have records you can search prior to your arrival. If possible, find the oldest Afri-can American or Black Woman buried in the cemetery. If your cemetery doesn't have any Black or African American people buried within, go to the grave of the oldest woman you can find.

Before you go to the cemetery, go to the sacred space you created for Marie Laveau and light your blue and white can-dles. Make your offering of salted water and tell her of what you are going to do. Ask for her protection while you do this work at the cemetery to call upon Manman Brijit for assistance.

The Divine Marie Laveau is the Higher Power we call upon before we do this work with Manman Brijit. As always in life, we have free will to decide what we will do and will not do. It is your decision to decide not to call upon Mama Marie before you perform this cemetery rite. *However,* I strongly encourage you to enlist the aid and support of Marie Laveau, as instructed, before you perform this cemetery rite with Manman Brijit.

As magickal, spiritual people, we should strive to remain humble and ask for the assistance of our Higher Powers and deities, goddesses and gods, when we seek to perform rites of powerful juju.

Items Needed

Coins to throw to the gatekeepers as you enter the cemetery

Small stones gathered from the cemetery

Copies of court papers and documents from the case you are working

An eggplant

A yam

A purple candle, a white candle, and a black candle (4-inch chime candles or birthday-size candles)

A cigar

A small bottle of rum

Coins of each denomination to leave at the gravesite

Timing

Whenever you need to do this work.

Ritual

Go to the cemetery. Upon entering, throw coins to the spiritual gatekeepers. Throwing coins is an offer of respect. It is your acknowledgment that you are entering their world, and you respect their power.

You can go anytime, day or night. But be careful! Doing rites in cemeteries is powerful work and, in some places, may be considered illegal. You will need to take ownership of your decision to do this work. However, in my experience, if you have called upon the protection of your deities and Marie Laveau and your work is true and sincere, you will be cloaked in the invisibility of Spirit while you work.

Once you are in the cemetery, gather several small stones as you make your way to the gravesite of the woman you are calling upon for assistance in the name of Manman Brijit. When you arrive at the grave, make a small pyramid out of the stones and slide the court papers under the stone pyramid.

A word about leaving court documents … unfortunately, a person's docket information is easily accessible online. If you know a person is due in court, all it takes is a simple search to find the courtroom, the date, and the time. Once you enter the US court system, a lot of your privacy flies right out the window. Someone discovering these copies won't further violate your privacy. So, don't be squeamish about leaving your documents for Manman Brijit. They will be sitting under your stone pyramid. You gotta have faith, baby.

Lay the eggplant and yam next to the stones. Place your candles in the dirt. Light the candles. Light the cigar. Put the lit end of the cigar in your mouth and blow. The smoke from the cigar will waft over the candles and the stone pyramid.

Tell the buried woman of your plight. Thank her and Manman Brijit for listening to your woes and prayers. Promise to return and honor the woman's grave (however you plan to do that—bringing fresh flowers is always ideal). Again, *don't make promises to the dead you can't keep!* The dead are deserving of respect and honor, and when you call upon them for assistance and they help you, you are obligated to honor your promises. Not doing so may bring unfavorable consequences your way.

Take a sip of rum. Blow the rum to the four directions (north, south, east, and west).

Turn and walk away. Leave all your offerings on the grave. I know you'll be tempted, but *do not look back.* Not looking back is your testament of faith. Go home by a different route. If you feel heady or out of your body, that is natural. You've just done a powerful rite. Take it easy. Be gentle with yourself. Take a shower or bath. Put on some fresh clothes. Eat some nourishing and comforting foods. And no matter how much it may press upon you, don't tell anyone about the work you have done. Let Manman Brijit and the buried woman work for you. Have faith.

When you know the outcome of the situation for which you did the work (no matter what that outcome may be—Spirit often has a way of working things out in its own way and time), return to the woman's grave, pay your respects, and leave your offering.

●●●●●●●●●●●●●●●●●●●

Creating a Sacred Space for Manman Brijit

It is my sincere desire for this work and image to not be confused with the Celtic Goddess Brigid. So, instead of a formal, dedicated space for Manman Brijit, I ask you to keep your pact with the woman upon whose grave you did your work. Your word is your bond.

However, we can still create a sacred space for Manman Brijit.

Items Needed

A dedicated candle for Manman Brijit (per the following instructions)

Image of Manman Brijit

Deep purple candle

Florida Water

A black cloth

Fresh flowers

For your dedicated candle to Manman Brijit, I recommend purchasing a candle for her (which you can do online or in person if you happen to be in New Orleans) through The Island of Salvation Botanica. A Google search will take you to their website. You can also print out an image of Manman Brijit—her face should be a Black Woman's face—and use it on your altar.

You could also use a deep purple candle to represent Manman Brijit. Cleanse the candle with Florida Water and set it upon a black cloth. Say a prayer of thanksgiving to Manman Brijit for helping you with your plight when you light the candle. A good time to light your candle is during the dark moon. You could also light your candle during the time of the ancestors, which we celebrate as Halloween, Samhain, or, as it is called in Vodou, Fet Ghede, which occurs October 31 through November 2.

Also, the woman's grave upon which you did your work is now a sacred space in your tool bag of powerful, good juju. Please return to the cemetery and lay fresh flowers upon her grave.

Keep this woman's name and spirit in your heart and in your prayers, daily. Remember and honor her. You can also pour water to her as described in the Ancestor Ritual in my previous book, *Good Juju*.

May the protection and blessings of Manman Brijit be with you and your loved ones.

calling on sekhmet for power

Song: "Circle of Life"
Artist: Tsidii Le Loka, *The Lion King* Ensemble,
Lebo M., and Faca Kulu

SEKHMET IS FIERCE. She is known as a goddess of war and
the daughter of Ra. Beer and pomegranate juices were used to
calm her when her rage became uncontrollable (Farrar 1987,
269). The Goddess Sekhmet is sometimes considered a dark
aspect of the Goddess Hathor, a major Egyptian goddess of
love and fertility. Sekhmet, like Hathor, is often depicted with
a flaming solar disk between two horns on her head. Sekhmet
is also frequently seen as a lion-headed goddess, which
is how she appeared when I gazed upon her in the
British Museum.

The power of Sekhmet is unfathomable and limitless. She is ancient. She is revered. One need only gaze upon her image to feel her influence.

Soul Speak

The British Museum, London, England, 2012.

I could barely look upon her. She took my breath away. So strong was her force, so gargantuan her power, that when I stumbled upon the statue of the Goddess Sekhmet in the British Museum in London, I had to back up three steps.

It took me several attempts to approach her. There she sat, regal upon her throne. I couldn't even approach her face-to-face. I was weak, stumbling, humbled, and scared. I had to creep around from the side of her statue to spiritually prostrate myself before her.

"Goddess Sekhmet, I know I am not worthy, but stand before you I do. Help me be strong and carry on. Grace me with your power, your love, your light. My path is dark. I cannot see the light. Weary am I of that which harms me. I am mortal. Please support me. Grant me your counsel, your guidance, your protection. Goddess Sekhmet, I am on my knees." I whispered to her as I stood before her grace and power in the British Museum. It didn't take much imagination to picture her in a golden temple, receiving those who dared bow before her!

How can a statue of stone sitting in a museum fill me with such awe and respect? Because Sekhmet comes from beyond time. She exists in the realm of Divine Feminine strength, admiration, and power. We *know* her. She scares us because she reminds us of who we are and what we have forgotten about ourselves, and how we have given away our power by playing small.

The Goddess Sekhmet won't let us play small. That's why she shook me to my core when I came upon her statue. In this world, we easily forget our goddess-given divinity as people of power. That we come from an ancestry of strong queens. That, once upon a time, we were revered and honored.

We need images of antiquity to remind us of who we truly are. We need to know deep in our bones that we are so much greater than those who seek to oppress us. It can be hard to rise above stereotypes and tropes that seek to keep us in places of weakness and victimhood. Those in power work hard to keep those they oppress beneath their feet. They know they sit on their false thrones because they have crushed the spirits of those they oppress. No more!

I called upon the Goddess Sekhmet because I was ready to walk a different path. We can call upon her when our soul cries out for change, but we have no idea where to begin or how to start. We can call upon her to bless us with strength, courage, and determination. We can call upon her to help us go the distance and change our lives.

"The Circle of Life" ~ Why I Chose This Song for Goddess Sekhmet

The opening call of "The Circle of Life" makes chills run up and down my spine. I want to stand and run through the tall

grass of an ancient African prairie, into the arms of my ancestors who are waiting for me, who whisper to me, "You done
good, girl. You done a good job."

I want to sit with them in their hut. I want them to stroke
my hair and bless me with unconditional love. I want them to
say, "Welcome home."

I want them to say, "We know you've been gone a long
time, but you're home now, and we're here for you. We've
always been with you, gazing down upon you from the starry
skies in the dark night. You have never been alone. We have
been and always shall be with you."

Oh, bless my African ancestors! I've never been to Africa.
But I would surmise I'm not alone in my feeling as an African
American, a Black Woman in America—many of us have had
the same dream, to be welcomed home, back to the land from
where our ancestors were forcibly taken and enslaved. We long
for a land where we belong. A land where our feet walk the
earth in peace. Where we can be home.

And that is exactly the feeling, the ancestral memory I
floated upon when I sat in the audience, watching *The Lion
King* Broadway musical. Such was its imprint upon my soul
that I saw it not once but twice, something I had never done
before. And the second time I saw it, I went by myself, which
was also a first-time experience for me: treating myself to a
Broadway musical, alone.

The first time I saw the musical, as I sat in pure joy enjoying the performance, I realized how much the theatre and the expression of creativity—the songs, dances, costumes, sets, lighting, the whole damn thing—filled my soul. And I had to question, "Why am I not doing this?"

At that time, I was stuck in a job I hated. I couldn't stand the organization I was working for. Every day was a struggle to pull myself out of bed and show up, and my disdain and the miserable working conditions were taking a toll on my mental health, well-being, and happiness.

But when I went to see *The Lion King*, I was filled with hope. I knew in my soul, sitting in that theatre, that a life in the creative arts was where I belonged. I knew I had to carry on and fulfill my dream of becoming a published author. I knew my dreams mattered, and they were important.

Such was the effect upon me that when I sat down to choose a song for the formidable Goddess Sekhmet—she who is fierce and determined, she who commands her throne, she who is the epitome of confidence and determination, she whose lion-headed face is encircled by a halo of power—I knew "The Circle of Life" was the right choice.

And if you've never seen the *Lion King* musical, there is a fantastic video on YouTube, "*The Lion King* Broadway Cast Takes Over NYC Subway and Sings 'Circle of Life.'" The video captures the cast performing "The Circle of Life" for subway passengers. What a treat!

●●●●●●●●●●●●●●●●●●

Ritual for Beseeching Sekhmet, the Lion-Headed Goddess

We call upon the Goddess Sekhmet to help us stand up. We ask her to help us realize we are indeed worthy, and our playing small is detrimental to our abilities—call forth and manifest!

Items Needed

Flat surface to serve as your altar for the ritual
Golden cloth
A piece of plastic wrap large enough to cover your
     working surface
Yellow taper candle
Florida Water
Olive oil
Golden glitter
Fireproof candleholder
Citrine
Fire agate
Amber resin
A square of brown paper
Fireproof container, such as a mini cauldron

Timing

Perform this ritual on a Sunday during the waxing moon cycle, when the moon is growing from the first crescent to the full moon. Although you will be performing this ritual during the day, we want to be sure you are doing it during the waxing cycle of the moon. The new moon is normally considered the dark moon, which means it cannot be seen in the night sky. Wait to perform this ritual until you have seen the moon in the night sky.

Ritual

On a Sunday at the hour of noon, during the waxing moon cycle, appeal to the Goddess Sekhmet to assist you with your plight.

Cover your flat surface with the golden cloth.

Lay down your plastic wrap. This will keep your altar cloth clean while you dress and fix your yellow candle.

Cleanse your yellow candle with Florida Water. Anoint it with olive oil. Sprinkle golden glitter upon your yellow candle. Stand your candle upright. Knock three times upon the candle, then tap the candle three times upon your altar. Say,

> *This candle is dressed in honor of the Goddess Sekhmet.*
> *Thank you, Goddess Sekhmet, for helping me.*

Discard your plastic wrap.

Place your candle in the fireproof candleholder. Place the citrine, fire agate, and amber resin around the base of your candleholder.

Now make the petition paper by tearing the sides of the brown paper so all four sides have torn edges. Write your prayers for courage, strength, and confidence on the brown paper. Try to use words that speak to your power as a living being who comes from a long line of powerful ancestors, such as, *I am worthy, I am an eternal being, I am a link—an unending chain of power and strength.*

Anoint the paper with five drops of olive oil in a five-spot pattern: place a drop of olive oil in the upper left corner of the paper, then continue clockwise, placing a drop of oil in all four corners of the paper. Finish by placing a drop of olive oil in the center of the paper.

Light your yellow candle.

Pick up your anointed petition paper. Say your prayer aloud. Then touch the paper to the flame of the burning candle. Place the burning petition paper in the fireproof container. Allow the paper to burn to ashes in the fireproof container. Once the ashes have cooled, bury them in your backyard or blow upon them and let the power of air carry them away.

Creating a Sacred Space for Sekhmet

You can connect with the power of the Goddess Sekhmet by creating a sacred space for her. To create your sacred space, use the golden altar cloth, citrine, fire agate, and amber resin from your ritual. Creating a sacred altar space for the Goddess Sekhmet, whom you have called upon to aid you, is a lovely, magickal way to keep her powerful presence in your life. You can leave the altar up for as long as you deem necessary. You can also create this sacred space without performing the ritual described; however, you will find the sacred space more meaningful once you have called upon the goddess to aid you in your troubles.

Items Needed

Golden altar cloth

Florida Water

Olive oil

Golden glitter

Yellow taper candle

Fireproof candleholder

Citrine, fire agate, and amber resin

Dress and fix a yellow candle as described in the Sekhmet ritual. Place your candle in a fireproof candleholder and arrange the stones and resin around the base of the candleholder. Light your candle during the waxing moon phase, on a Sunday, at the hour of noon, to connect to the power of your ritual and the benevolence of the Goddess Sekhmet. Spend time before your flame in prayer and reverence. When finished, pinch out your candle flame.

In time, as your relationship with Sekhmet grows, you may find yourself adding lion figurines or other items that signify power and strength to your sacred space. Let your imagination carry you to the plains of Africa. Allow the spirit of the ancient ones to be your guide as you adorn your sacred space dedicated to the Goddess Sekhmet.

seven

calling on tituba for help being yourself

Song: "Precious"
Artist: Esperanza Spalding

TITUBA REMAINS AN ENIGMA and a mystery. Very little is known about her life, but we know she played an integral part in the Salem Witch Trials. We know she was a woman of dark skin. Research suggests she may have been an Arawak or a West Indian woman of African heritage. What is readily accepted is that Tituba was an enslaved woman who cast a powerful spell onto the Salem Witch Trials. It is also known that after Tituba took the stand during the Salem Witch Trials, she spent many months in prison and was freed by an anonymous donor.

Why is Tituba included as one of twelve powerful goddesses featured in my book? Because Tituba has been relegated to the dark and dusty corners of the Craft. As an African American practicing Witch, there is little iconography that looks like me or feels like me when it comes to American Witchcraft practices.

When I visited Salem in the 1990s, I took a tour that brought me face-to-face with a plastic mannequin of Tituba. I was revolted by the display. Tituba was dressed in ragged clothes. She wore the most gawd-awful Afro wig on her head, and her lips were painted bright red. It disgusted me.

There is little historical data available for Tituba. For years I've searched for factual data concerning her life, her birth, or any tidbit outside what was recorded in the history of the Salem Witch Trials of 1692. Such it is. Anything written about Tituba's life, outside of what would fill two paragraphs, is all fiction and speculation.

Searching genealogical databases for information on enslaved African Americans is a harsh and daunting experience. Records of our people simply aren't there the way they are for people of European ancestry in the United States of America. When your ancestors were regarded as chattel, little importance is given to where they came from or what their real names were. In fact, scant records exist outside a first name, which was given by slaveowners, or perhaps a surname, which was also given by slaveowners. A testament to how enslaved Africans were deemed the property of the slaveowner.

It is traditionally accepted that the birthplace of Tituba was Barbados. She was married to John Indian, and they resided in Salem, Massachusetts, most significantly during the year 1692. Tituba was an enslaved Woman of Color to the Samuel Parris household.

I would like to suggest the reading of *I, Tituba, Black Witch of Salem* by Maryse Condé, which is a wonderful historical, fictional account of Tituba's life. Maryse Condé's book gives great insight into Tituba's possible childhood and her adult life in Salem.

Black Women, African American women, are at the heart and soul of the United States. Our blood, sweat, and tears run deep into the soil, the veins, and the waters of this land. As a Witch, Tituba deserves her due. She needs to be honored, uplifted, and respected.

Soul Speak

Salem, Massachusetts! Salem, Massachusetts, is considered a pilgrimage for Witches and anyone interested in the Occult, history, and the lore of Witchcraft.

While New Orleans holds its special charm for Hoodoo and Vodou, Salem holds its charm for Witchcraft and infamy for the Witch Trials of 1692. Pretty much every Witch I've known wants to visit Salem, especially during the sacred time of Samhain or the festive celebration of Halloween. I've visited Salem twice. It is an otherworldly place. As a practicing Witch, when you walk the cobbled streets and visit all the great stores and shops, you feel as if you've come home. Salem is a place where you can let your Witch flag fly! And if you're a history buff, Salem has a plethora of history and a cauldron of knowledge just waiting to be explored.

But one cannot talk about Salem or the trials of 1692 without paying respect to Tituba.

Tituba became the catalyst for the Salem Witch Trials when she was arrested, imprisoned, and called to testify. After she was freed from prison, she seemed to disappear into a cloud of magickal smoke.

"Precious" ~ Why I Chose This Song for Goddess Tituba

In the song "Precious," Esperanza Spalding sings about divine energy and not being ashamed of who we are. She tells us not to apologize for our identities, and if folks can't or don't understand us, it's their problem, not ours.

Tituba was caught in a trap. She was an enslaved Woman of Color, beaten and made to confess to crimes she did not do. And yet, somehow, Tituba was able to use her wits, her intelligence, to spin a tale so beyond the imaginations of the Puritan environment to which she was bound and tap into the fear running rampant in Salem, Massachusetts, in 1692.

Per Famous-Trials.com, "The matter might have ended with admonishments were it not for Tituba. After first adamantly denying any guilt, afraid perhaps of being made a scapegoat, Tituba claimed that she was approached by a tall man from Boston—obviously Satan—who sometimes appeared as a dog or a hog and who asked her to sign in his book and to do his work.

Yes, Tituba declared, she was a witch, and moreover she and four other witches, including Good and Osborne, had flown through the air on their poles. She had tried to run to Reverend Parris for counsel, she said, but the devil had blocked her path" (2021).

And although this chapter focuses on Tituba, our compassionate hearts cannot forget the women and men who were falsely accused of Witchcraft—hanged from the gallows, and one poor man pressed to death—because people of the time believed them to be Witches, which is apparently the most heinous thing any woman or man can be accused of being.

On another trip to Salem, Massachusetts, in the 1990s, we got swept up into the mock trial for Bridget Bishop. Bridget Bishop was a white woman accused of Witchcraft and the first person hanged for her "crimes." My husband and I were enjoying our time in Salem on a beautiful fall afternoon when we were jarred from the magic by an utterly surreal and disturbing moment. The sounds of taunting and name-calling permeated the air. A young woman dressed in period clothing was encircled by others dressed in period clothing. She was being accused of Witchcraft as she stood on the cobbled sidewalk.

Of course, this was a reenactment the city of Salem provides for tourists, but as a practicing Witch, it was heart-wrenching! We followed the actors into the Salem courthouse, where we paid a fee to participate in the trial of Bridget Bishop. My husband and I sat in the jury box, and I silently wept when they brought "Bridget Bishop," handcuffed in shackles, before the magistrate. It was a chilling experience.

The reenactment offered those who were in the court the chance to cross-examine witnesses and decide whether Bridget was guilty or not guilty. Of course, I loudly proclaimed her innocence! And as I passed through the doors of the courthouse, back into the light of reality, the actress who played Bridget whispered "thank you" to me.

Contrary to the young woman portraying her, Bridget Bishop was actually in her late fifties or possibly even sixty years old when she was hanged for being a Witch. The same age I am now, as I write these words, which is even more disturbing!

Why? Why are people so afraid of Witches? Why do they fear us?

Fear is a powerful thing. It can twist and turn reality into something so bizarre, one doesn't know which way is up or down. Fear can be used to make people conform, spout beliefs and support practices they don't believe in, and honor their ancestral religions and practices behind closed doors or in secret. It can force people into taking risks so great that, if found out, they could be persecuted or lose their children, jobs, or families.

I have a few thoughts on why people fear Witches, who for the most part are *women*. These thoughts are my own, and I take ownership of them.

It is no secret patriarchal societies have sought to oppress women since time immemorial. We're underpaid and undervalued. If we stand up for ourselves, we're called a "bitch," or, even worse, a "witch."

Women are made to feel bad about their menstrual cycles —that menstruation's a curse. We should seek to get rid of it, to hide our bleeding, and we certainly shouldn't complain about it if we feel bad or need time off from work for our "monthlies." In some spiritual societies, women are shunned from taking part in rituals when they are on their periods. And women suffer tremendously with dis-eases emanating from our reproductive organs, which can be misdiagnosed for years, causing needless suffering and pain. All sorts of nasty words are attached to a woman's most powerful body parts, words used to degrade, shame, and devalue. Yet it is a woman's vagina that allows a human being entry into the physical world.

Women have traditionally been healers, tapping into intuitive or hereditary knowledge of healing plants and the agriculture of their homelands to aid, heal, and comfort. And women are innately *spiritual*. We nurture, we care, we comfort, we cry. The soul of the Universe courses within us and through us. We are powerful, and men know it.

Want to take away a culture? Persecute the women.

Esperanza Spalding's song "Precious" is a call to us—all of us, with our Witch abilities, intuitions, deep feelings, and inner knowing, whether we are out of the broom closet or not. For even in this time and age, it's not safe for everyone to declare they are a Witch.

However, I am glad for all the coming-out on social media and hashtags such as #witchesofinstagram, #blackgirlmagic, #magick, and #witchlifestyle, which let people know they are not alone.

●●●●●●●●●●●●●●●●●●

As We Remember and Honor Tituba, We Strengthen and Empower Ourselves

Tituba is a mirror into the past lives of those who align with the word *Witch*. We may be out of the broom closet, or we may be Witches secretly in our hearts, cherishing our solitude and private practices. By remembering and honoring Tituba, we strengthen and empower ourselves to be spiritual, magickal, Witchy practitioners.

Items Needed

> White candle
>
> Florida Water
>
> Blessing oil
>
> Fireproof candleholder
>
> Witch cake (any sweet pastry or cake that you designate as a Witch cake; if you feel called to bake your own, all the better)*
>
> *Note that the Witch cake described in historical documents contained urine (called "waters") and was used to discover Witches so they could be persecuted. We are not using our cake in that manner. Our cake is an offering of gratitude for Witches.
>
> Black onyx stone (said to help one walk the path alone and become a master of their destiny)
>
> Salt

Timing

Since much about Tituba's life remains a mystery, one of the best things we can do is keep her in our memory, especially around October 31. While many of the rituals in my book can be done at any time in the year, I suggest we perform this ritual for Tituba during the autumn season, around the time of Samhain and Halloween.

Ritual

Cleanse your white candle with Florida Water and anoint it with a blessing oil of your choice. Place the candle in a fireproof candleholder and set it aside.

Carve a *W* into your pastry or cake to designate it as your Witch cake.

Light your candle.

Hold the black onyx stone and Witch cake in your hands. Say,

> *Dear Tituba, you may be gone, but you shall never be*
> *forgotten. We remember you, honor you, and cherish*
> *you for your courage and contribution to our history.*
> *Please accept our offerings of love and gratitude.*

Place your Witch cake and stone in front of the candle. Make a ring of salt around the candle, cake, and stone. Allow the candle to burn all the way out. When finished, gather up the salt and throw it out your front door. Bury the cake and place your stone on your sacred space for Tituba.

❋❋❋❋❋❋❋❋❋❋❋❋❋❋❋❋❋❋

Creating a Sacred Space for Tituba

After you have completed your ritual for the Goddess Tituba, you may want to connect with her on a regular basis, outside of the ritual described. Creating a sacred altar space for the goddess you have called upon to aid you is a lovely, magickal way to keep her powerful presence in your life. You can leave the altar up for as long as you deem necessary. You can also create this sacred space without performing the ritual described; however, you will find the sacred space more meaningful once you have called upon the goddess to aid you in your troubles.

Please understand that the creation of sacred space for Tituba is what came to me through my heart, love, and detailed research about her life. I pray it brings honor to her and enlightenment to all who read of her in this book.

Items Needed

Florida Water

Altar cloth (use a color or pattern that is pleasing to you)

Shea butter

A beautiful piece of fabric

Miniature shoes

Fresh flowers

White candle

Fireproof candleholder

Black onyx stone

Let us create a sacred space for Tituba that shows we love and appreciate her as a *woman* for whom the most basic of things would have been a far cry from her daily life.

Shea butter is used because Tituba was beaten. Shea butter would have been a welcome soothing ointment to her skin. Shea butter is available at health food stores and online through sellers of natural products. Try to purchase shea butter that is certified "fair trade" and "organic." With a little research, you may be able to purchase shea butter from organizations that support African women.

A beautiful piece of fabric is included because she could have used this to make herself some pretty clothes.

The shoes can be "miniature" shoes from a hobby store, to signify she had good shoes to wear on her feet. Shoes are a necessary piece of clothing many of us probably take for granted or have a love affair or obsession with. I, too, love shoes. But imagine Tituba, an enslaved woman, wearing rags or no shoes on her feet.

Designate your sacred space for Tituba. Cleanse the space with Florida Water and cover it with a cloth that is pleasing to your eye. Set all your items upon the cloth. Whenever you feel called to her, and/or especially during Samhain or Halloween, light your candle for Tituba, and give her fresh flowers. Once the flowers begin to wilt, dispose of them either by laying them next to a tree or simply upon the earth.

eight
HEALING YOUR SOUL
WITH SULIS MINERVA

Song: "Ball and Chain"
Artist: Janis Joplin

SULIS MINERVA WAS THE goddess of the baths named Aquae Sulis. The Romans discovered the baths and learned of their Celtic history (herstory) of healing powers and worship to the Goddess Sulis. The Romans, as was their custom, syncretized this goddess with one of their own and brought their names together: *Sulis* and *Minerva*.

People would come to the baths to heal and make offerings to the Goddess Sulis Minerva. Not only would people drop coins to Sulis Minerva, but they would also leave "curse tablets," asking her to curse those who had harmed them or done them wrong!

Soul Speak

Oh, for the love of hot water!

In September 2012, I fulfilled a lifelong dream, which was to travel to London, England. I had dreamed of traveling to London since I was a child, having been smitten by the spell so heavily cast by the movie *Mary Poppins*. I just had to get to London, someway, somehow!

And so, in my fifty-second year of life, along with my faithful and loving traveling companion, my husband, we both for the first time in our lives set foot upon British soil and arrived in the city of London.

Immediately, I felt at home. Everything I had dreamed about seeing—red telephone booths, flats, the tube/underground—was there. Just to hear people speaking in British accents was music to my ears. I was overjoyed that this long-held dream had manifested.

We had planned quite an itinerary for ourselves, which, of course, included seeing the famous Portobello Road, made popular in the movie *Bedknobs and Broomsticks*, another Witchy favorite, and all the other regular tourist stops. But somewhere along the way, we added a trip to Bath, England.

Perhaps our guidebook had suggested it? Or maybe the Goddess was afoot, whispering in our ears? I can't quite remember how we decided to go to Bath. But it was one of the highlights of our first trip to England.

I can clearly remember the excitement of boarding the train from London's Piccadilly Circus station for the ride to Bath. It was a clear, sunny day. As we rode the train, we were amazed at the green countryside. The green was so luscious! It just seemed to go on forever!

As the train pulled into Bath, we marveled at the town, the houses, and shops. It was truly a step back in time.

After we disembarked from the train, we walked along the river and came to a roaring wall of water. It took our breath away. The water was so powerful. The day was so clear. The stonework of Bath was gorgeous. It was as if we were in a living dream.

We arrived in the town square proper and were given instructions as to what sites we may like to see, and when to meet up again in the square for departure. I could have stayed in Bath forever. It truly fulfilled all my magickal thoughts of what I had dreamed an English countryside town to be.

Hubby and I immediately took off on our own, as we love to do. We don't mind going with a group to tour places we've never been, but we don't like to hang with the group if it's possible to strike out on our own.

As we wandered through town, we saw signs pointing toward the baths.

Now, let me tell you, I love hot springs. Hubby and I have crisscrossed our home state of Colorado, taking advantage of all the wonderful hot springs our beautiful, mountainous state has to offer. There is nothing better than immersing my body in a deep pool of healing mineral water. Even just writing those words relaxes my mind, body, and spirit.

Our time in Bath was limited, so we knew we couldn't actually take a bath *(waaah!)*, but we made our way to the Roman baths anyway. We had to see this legendary place.

As we approached the baths, we could see a ring of statues. The baths are lined with Roman sculptures surrounding the high walls. We looked down from above and saw a pool of water. The light casting beams upon the water was otherworldly. It was magick. We were so happy when we learned we could tour the bath.

We paid our admission price and set out on our self-guided tour. Down we went into the underground. It was dimly lit. Museum cases lined the pathway, telling the history of the bath, and as we wound our way through the pathways, I came face-to-face with a large head in glass case. It was the bust of Sulis Minerva.

I had never known anything about her. But there she was, gazing down upon us. Next to the glass-encased bust of Sulis Minerva was a display of what the baths had looked like in all their splendor during Roman times. Not far from the display was a small opening where you could look and see the original place where the waters of the spring emanated from, and where pilgrims would have walked to leave their offerings.

Oh, how I wanted to live during those times! Oh, how I wanted to be a priestess in the temple of the Goddess Sulis Minerva! How I longed to live during a time when the worship of the Divine Feminine was a normal part of everyday life, and not something looked upon with scorn and disdain!

I could feel those ancient peoples coming to the baths in total faith, believing, knowing, that the Goddess Sulis Minerva would hear their prayers and help them.

I could have stayed in the underground waterways of Goddess Sulis Minerva forever, but alas, we had to move on. We didn't want to miss our train back to London. As we emerged from our self-guided tour, there was a wonderful little gift shop. I bought a small signed replica of the bust of the Goddess Sulis Minerva, and she's been with me ever since that magickal trip to Bath, England.

"Ball and Chain" ~ Why I Chose This Song for Goddess Sulis Minerva

Unlike every other song listed for the powerful goddesses in this book, this is the only song I want you to listen to via the video on YouTube. The title of the video is "Janis Joplin—Ball & Chain—Monterey Pop" (CriterionCollection).

Even though "Ball and Chain" exists as a downloadable song, there is no other version of this song, sung by the immortal and incredible Janis Joplin, that conveys the power that is contained in this video. It was filmed when she burst upon the music scene at the Monterey Pop Jazz Festival in 1967.

There, Janis stands in her golden threads, belting out her heart, a true goddess herself, spinning her magick, singing about the rain and the torment of heartache to the amazement and awe of all who were blessed to see her that legendary day.

One of the best things about the video is the sheer awe on Mama Cass Elliot's face. If you look closely, you can see Mama

Cass is wearing a cameo ring and a butterfly ring. Both are symbols of women and transformation. For those present, listening, and watching, Janis Joplin was a transformative experience.

Just as people were transformed and transported through the powerful sounds of Janis Joplin's voice, transformation is why people of ancient times came to the waters of Goddess Sulis Minerva. They needed healing. They needed regeneration. And so, they brought their woes and worries and bodies to her waters.

Water cleanses us, blesses us, renews us, and refreshes us. In my prayers to my ancestors every morning, I say, *From water we all come, and unto water we all must return.*

During troubled times, water, especially hot mineral water, heals your soul. If you can't make it to a hot spring, a long soak does wonders, and even a long hot shower can ease your troubles and bring healing to your mind, body, and spirit.

Water calms us as the sound of ocean waves ebbing back and forth upon the shoreline. Water relaxes us as the sound of rain upon a window. Water gets our attention when its harbinger, thunder, crackles across the sky. The sound of water is so healing, calming, and relaxing, there are even applications you can download to bring its tranquility into your life.

Janis Joplin is anything but calm in her video "Ball and Chain." Her soul-shattering voice and power, her musical genius, quake upon your troubles and take your spirit to a place where it can be healed. Let her healing power of music flow into and over you. Let her cries carry your troubles to the healing waters of the Goddess Sulis Minerva, for surely her voice is powerful juju for troubled times.

Wash Us, Free Us from Ourselves Ritual

For this ritual, I ask you to cleanse yourself with the healing properties of a bath or a long hot shower. I ask you to carve out a time when you will not be disturbed.

Items Needed

A white candle

Florida Water

Fireproof candleholder

Epsom salts (scented or unscented)

Small container to hold water (if you are taking a shower)

Clean clothes (a fresh robe or pajamas or fresh clothes for the day)

Timing

As needed.

Ritual

When you are ready for your bath, cleanse your candle with Florida Water. Place your candle in the fireproof candleholder.

Light your candle.

Pour one cup of the Epsom salts into the bottom of the tub and allow the tub to fill with warm water (a comfortable temperature). Epsom salt originated in England in the town of Epsom, located in Surrey. If you are taking a shower, pour a small amount of Epsom salt into a container and carry it into the shower with you.

Draw your bath.

Enter your bath or shower.

Allow the healing water of your bath or shower to relax you. As you relax, bring to mind thoughts of Sulis Minerva. Tell her of your troubles. Talk openly and sincerely to her.

If you are taking a shower, when you have finished speaking with Goddess Sulis Minerva, thank her for listening to your woes. Fill the container with warm water and pour the salted water over your body.

If you are taking a bath, scoop some of your bathwater into your hands and pour water over your body several times.

Emerge from your bath.

If you can, allow your body to air-dry. This way, you won't towel off all the magick you've just created.

If your candle is still burning, you can snuff or pinch it out and save it for the next time you choose to perform this ritual. If your candle has burned all the way down, just cleanse and prepare a new candle the next time you perform this ritual.

Put on fresh clothes. If you're heading to bed, your clothes can be a fresh robe or clean pajamas, or simply your clean naked self, if you prefer it that way.

If you're heading out for the day, put on fresh, clean clothes. Putting on fresh, clean clothes carries the power of your healing magick with you. You've just cleansed your mind, body, and spirit. Keep the good juju by wearing fresh, clean clothes.

If you're going to bed, I wish you sweet, healing dreams. May you rest well and awaken to bright beginnings.

If you are setting out for the day, may all be well with you. May you feel the power of good juju all around you.

❋❋❋❋❋❋❋❋❋❋❋❋❋❋❋❋❋❋❋

Creating a Sacred Space for Sulis Minerva

After you have completed your ritual for the Goddess Sulis Minerva, you may want to connect with her on a regular basis, outside of the ritual described. Creating a sacred altar space for the goddess you have called upon to aid you is a lovely, magickal way to keep her powerful presence in your life. You can leave the altar up for as long as you deem necessary. You can also create this sacred space without performing the ritual described; however, you will find the sacred space more meaningful once you have the called upon the goddess to aid you in your troubles.

On our tour of the Roman baths, we wound our way through the underground display of priceless museum objects, all set against the backdrop of running water from the hot spring. I came upon a plaque that read as follows:

> "The Temple of Sulis Minerva. The Temple stood here with its Gorgon's head pediment, facing the open courtyard and great altar. Only three of the steps that led up to the Temple can be seen. The pagan Temple may have been destroyed by Christians in the 7th century when a monastery was founded at Bath."

The gorgon's head is a massive stone face that graces the opening of the temple. It is a masculine face that reminds me of the sun.

As we continued our tour, I came across another plaque:

"Luna and Sol from the Temple Courtyard. Faced each other across the great altar from buildings in the Temple Courtyard. The Luna pediment rose above the reconstructed building to the left, which may have served as a special place for the sick to seek a cure with divine help."

What stands out most to me from the quotes on the plaques are the words *pagan Temple* and *divine help*.

So, far back in ancient times, *Pagans*—which is still a loaded word, even in our world today—came to the temple of Sulis Minerva seeking divine help! How has the word *Pagan* come to mean someone who doesn't believe in a Higher Power?

Etymologically speaking, *Pagan* means "country dweller." As far back as the seventh century, country dwellers made pilgrimages to the goddess for divine healing when they were sick! They believed in a Higher Power.

Let us create a sacred space for Goddess Sulis Minerva with the intention of honoring her ancient memory, as a place one went to for divine healing to help with sickness and to avenge wrongs.

Items Needed

Soothing sounds of rain or running water

A printed image of the bust of Sulis Minerva (easily found through a Google search)

A piece of white chalk

A nice cup to serve as a chalice

A small amount of water in a container

Coins (preferably coins with a woman's face; you could
  also use chocolate gold coins)
A flat surface to use as your sacred space

Gather all your items. Pick a time when you will not be
disturbed or interrupted.

Play your water music. Allow the soothing sound of water
to relax your mind, body, and spirit. Gaze upon your printed
image of the Goddess Sulis Minerva. When you feel connected
with her, turn over your printed image and use your chalk to
write your feelings, thoughts, or healing intentions upon the
back of the paper. When you have finished writing, rub your
chalk words into the paper. When you do this, you have effec-
tively moved your words into Spirit, and no one will ever be
able to read what you have written!

Turn the paper over so you are once again looking at the
face of Sulis Minerva.

Set your chalice upon the image.

Cup your container of water.

Say,

Blessed be element of water.
Water that cleanses us, revives us, and heals us.

Pour a small amount of water into the chalice.

Hold your coins in your hands.

Take a moment to focus on the words you wrote on the
paper.

Take a deep breath and breathe out over the coins.

If your coins are made of metal, drop them into the chalice. If you're using chocolate coins, place them around the base of the chalice.

Say,

> *Dea Sulis Minerva* [which means "to the Goddess Sulis Minerva"], *from across the waters of time, I offer my words and coins to you. Thank you for hearing what lies upon my heart. Thank you for receiving my offering. I remember you. I honor your healing energies. I thank you.*

Take a moment to sit with the sacred space you have created. When you feel ready, tidy up your space. You can either leave the space up, if it is safe for you do so, or you can put your things away until you feel called to perform the ritual again. If you leave the space up, simply allow the water to evaporate. If you are taking the space down, pour the water outside upon the earth.

nine
fiNdiNG New beGiNNiNGS with NiNa simoNe

Song: "Feeling Good"
Artist: Nina Simone

AT ONE POINT DURING her career, Nina Simone was referred to as the High Priestess of Soul. As one worthy of that title, she is an icon, a goddess, and someone I feel deserves recognition, honor, and remembering.

For this chapter, I read Nina Simone's autobiography *I Put a Spell on You*, as well as several articles. I perused books about her life and watched countless videos, including the Netflix documentary *What Happened, Miss Simone?*

I learned through her own writing and my research about her life that she was very lonely. I know she was a perfectionist and held herself to extremely high standards. She ended up out there on the front lines of the Civil Rights Movement, but her true dream was to be recognized as a classical pianist. She was heartbroken when that dream fell through as a young woman. And although she ended up playing lots of jazz music, she never wanted to be considered a blues artist. She just did what she had to do to survive and went where her art took her. And being the passionate singer and artist and Black Woman she was, she had to get involved in the movement. Just listen to "Mississippi Goddam," and you'll know what I'm talking about.

Miss Nina, who was born Eunice Kathleen Waymon in Tryon, North Carolina, on February 21, 1933, changed her name to Nina Simone when she got her first gig playing in a nightclub. She changed her name to protect herself and shield her mother from finding out she was playing "real music," as her mother, who was a minister, called it. She took the name Nina from a nickname a boyfriend called her. He was actually calling her *niña,* which means "little girl" in Spanish. She took the name Simone from the gifted and talented French actor Simone Signoret.

Simone Signoret tore up the silver screen in the famous movie *Room at the Top*, released in 1959 by Romulus Films. If you're a movie buff, you can't go wrong with this film. It is indeed a classic in cinematography. If you'd like to touch with Nina Simone in a different way, set aside some time to watch this film. It's an eerie experience. You can clearly see how Simone Signoret may have influenced Nina Simone. Watching this movie is a nice way to connect with something she may have enjoyed.

Other interesting tidbits: She liked iced coffee and coffee ice cream (which is my favorite flavor of ice cream). She once danced naked in a nightclub in Liberia, Africa, and she participated in a three-day ritual, prescribed by an African Witch Doctor, which included a bone reading to reconcile with her father, who had passed away. The healing worked, and her father became a comforting, guiding spirit to her. In her autobiography, she mentions no one in Africa thought her ritual was strange, or thought she was strange when she spoke about it. When I learned she had participated in this ritual, I felt she'd have appreciated me as a practicing African American Witch!

Nina Simone was victim to a nasty, abusive husband, who was also her manager. She had major conflicts with men who didn't understand her and sought to control her life as a performer. It is also well documented she fought her own demons when the world got too heavy.

Miss Nina knew about troubled times. She not only sang about them, but she also lived them. Nina Simone passed away April 21, 2003. Her final resting place is Carry-le-Rouet, France. I pray in death she found the freedom she so desperately sought as a human being on Earth. I thank her for being someone we can turn to for help during our own troubled times.

Soul Speak

I was four years old, living in Columbus, Ohio, when the Civil Rights Movement marches began to take full speed. I was seven years old, living in Los Angeles, California, when Dr. Martin Luther King Jr. was shot and killed.

I was a child when these very important and significant events in the history and culture of American society were taking place.

I was too young to really understand what was going on, but these events permeated my life and left their mark on my soul. At that time, we referred to ourselves as Black. The words African American were not part of our everyday lingo. The word *Negro* was still around and in use, but thankfully its place in everyday vocabulary was waning. We were Black Folks, and I still refer to myself as a Black Woman.

So why is Nina Simone important to me?

Nina Simone's music was one of the background tracks to my childhood. Her music played on the turntable, and her albums were prominent in the living room. I am pleased to see vinyl and turntables, or record players, are making a comeback. Personally, I have a priceless set of vinyl records. I have a record player, which was a gift from my son. I love digging out my albums, pulling a shiny black vinyl record from its protective sleeve, placing it on the record player, and lowering the needle. That is a thrill and experience you just don't get with digital music! Yes, I am a bit of an audiophile.

Nina's strength, her courage, and her determination are definitely a touchstone for us in these days. When we are weary, tired, battle-fatigued, we can listen to her music and gaze at her dressed in her beautiful gowns and African wear. We can call upon her strength and power to help us in troubled times, whether those times are of a personal, universal, or global nature.

Things are happening for us, too, in modern times: we've seen the #MeToo movement come through, Women's Marches, the gay community fight for their civil rights, and a landmark Supreme Court ruling whose foundation stands on the shoulders of the Civil Rights Movement. And sadly, we've watched the killing of George Floyd, as well as the deaths of Breonna Taylor and Elijah McClain, bring people out into the streets, demanding justice and police reform. The United States has the most people incarcerated on the planet, of which the highest percentage is young African American/Black Men. And if that wasn't enough, the political climate is horrendous and social media allows bullying and harassment at levels never before experienced.

Also, as I sit and write these words, we are living through the COVID-19 pandemic, which is definitely a troubled time, something none of us have ever been through. We need people who are icons of strength, hope, and courage. I know Nina Simone's music is a balm for us. She had so much courage and strength. Even when she was dead-dog tired, afraid, or lonely and sad, she got out there. She still played. She played her music, and she played it her way. She was famous for not beginning a concert until the audience had quieted down.

Let us allow Miss Simone to help us find our own way by calling upon the power in her music and in her life. Let us honor her as the goddess she was and the influence she continues to be. May she lend us some of her powerful juju, which certainly was a help during troubled times, especially during the Civil Rights Movement in the United States, and for these troubled times we live in now.

"Feeling Good" ~ Why I Chose This Song for Goddess Nina Simone

Nina Simone begins singing "Feeling Good" without the accompaniment of her sacred piano. Her a cappella voice is clear as a bell, ringing across time, telling us it's a new day and a new dawn. Our ears can hear this must have been a new day and a new dawn for her, too, when she recorded this tremendous, inspiring, and uplifting piece of music. "Feeling Good" was recorded in 1965.

When I sat down to write this piece, it was indeed a new day and a new dawn. It was the new moon, which ushers in the beginning cycle of increase and abundance.

I always feel better and lighter at the beginning of a new or dark moon. It is called the dark moon because it will still be a few nights before the shining silver crescent appears in the sky.

Even though Nina Simone was known for her top hits such as "Porgy" and "I Put a Spell on You," which would seem the natural choice for this book, I chose "Feeling Good" because it deeply speaks to Miss Simone's drive, her need to be in control of her own life, and her desire to be *free* to rise above the troubled times that haunted her and her entire career.

A New Day Dawns Ritual

When I set out to conduct research on the life and experiences of Nina Simone, I found myself deeply touched by her struggles. Plan the timing of your ritual so you can be with the new day, right before the sun rises, when the sky is still dark.

Items Needed
A white candle
Florida Water
A bowl of water
Fireproof candleholder

Timing
Dark hour before sunrise during the new moon.

Ritual
Gather all your items and go somewhere you will not be disturbed. If it is possible for you to get outside, all the better.

Cleanse your white candle with the Florida Water by wiping the candle from the center up, including the wick, saying, *As above.* Then wipe the candle downward from the center with the Florida Water, saying, *As below.*

Add a few drops of Florida Water to your bowl of water.

Light your candle and place it in the fireproof candleholder. Place the bowl of water in front of the candle. Say,

Today is a New Moon and new beginning for me.
I am free. I am light. I am blessed, cleansed, and

refreshed. I look forward to this new day and this
new cycle for me. Blessed be. So mote it be.

Clap your hands three times.

Dip your fingers into the water. Sprinkle a few drops of water upon the top of your head. Sit quietly. Allow the blessing of your water and your words to permeate your being as you gaze into the candle flame.

Pinch out the candle and save it for the sacred space you will create for Nina Simone. Whenever you choose to repeat this ritual, you can take the candle from the sacred space and return it when you are done. When the candle gets close to burning out, you can use it to light another candle. Be sure to cleanse your new candle with Florida Water as previously instructed. That way you carry the good and powerful juju from each ritual you perform over to the next one.

You can dispose of the water in several ways. You can save the water and pour it over yourself in your morning bath or shower. Or you can pour the water onto the earth in your backyard or in your garden or down your front steps.

You can repeat this ritual every new moon or anytime you feel the need to bless and cleanse yourself. If you choose to do the ritual outside of the new moon, you can change the words of the ritual by saying,

Today [or Tonight] is a new beginning for me.
I am free. I am light. I am blessed, cleansed,

*and refreshed. I look forward to this new
beginning for me. Blessed be. So mote it be.*

Finish by clapping your hands three times.

****

Creating a Sacred Space for Nina Simone

After you have completed your ritual for the Goddess Nina Simone, you may want to connect with her on a regular basis, outside of the ritual described. Creating a sacred altar space for the goddess you have called upon to aid you is a lovely, magickal way to keep her powerful presence in your life. You can leave the altar up for as long as you deem necessary. You can also create this sacred space without performing the ritual described; however, you will find the sacred space more meaningful once you have the called upon the goddess to aid you in your troubles.

Items Needed

A white candle

Fireproof candleholder

A piece of African cloth

A pair of fabulous costume earrings (have fun shopping at thrift stores)

A song by Nina Simone that calls to you

A note about the word *Miss*. The word *Miss* is used as a title of respect in the Black community. It doesn't refer to someone's marital status. I, too, have been referred to as Miss Najah.

Miss Simone loved looking good. She was a glamorous, sexy dresser. She loved leopard prints and African clothing. She loved gowns and never took the stage looking anything less than her queenly self.

In her autobiography, Nina Simone wrote vividly of her love and the freedom she felt when she lived in the country of Liberia on the continent of Africa.

Find a small area where you can set up your items. Place the candle in its fireproof candleholder on the cloth. Set the earrings next to the candle.

Light the candle.

Spend a few moments listening to your song. Close your eyes and let her powerful voice take you to that place of courage, strength, and healing. When you are ready, open your eyes. Say a sincere prayer of thanks for the life of Nina Simone and the blessings she left us. Pinch out your candle.

You can spend time in this sacred space whenever you feel called to it. There is no wrong or right way to do it. It is there for you whenever you need it.

ten

HEALING HEARTBREAK
with NANCY WILSON

Song: "Guess Who I Saw Today"
Artist: Nancy Wilson

NANCY WILSON WAS BORN in Chillicothe, Ohio, and she lived in Columbus, Ohio. I also lived in Columbus until I was four years old. That would have been the year 1964. I have very few memories of that time and place, except what I see in old photos and the gossamer memories that flit through my mind. But I do know it was the time of great lounge singers.

Jazz was hot. Jazz was cool, and Nancy Wilson was an icon for Black households. She was *class.* She portrayed an image Black Women and Men desperately needed at the time. She showed us Black glamour. Something we still need as we aspire to rise above the muck of daily living. Nancy Wilson was like a dream in technicolor on her album covers, dressed in her beautiful clothes. Sometimes I like to pretend that maybe, had things been different or I'd been born at a different time, I would have been one of those smoky lounge singers, too.

"Guess Who I Saw Today" was Nancy Wilson's signature song. In fact, it was her debut song. And no one can sing it like Nancy Wilson.

During her life, she participated in the Selma to Montgomery marches. She was known as an activist and was awarded a star on the Hollywood Walk of Fame in 1990. She was known to be an impeccable dresser and a fashion icon. She was deeply connected to her family, so much so that she arranged her tour schedule around her family obligations.

Nancy Wilson passed away on December 13, 2018, in Pioneertown, California. She retained her classiness throughout her entire life and musical career. I know we're all about healthy living these days, and even though I've never been a cigarette smoker, I long for those smoke-filled jazz clubs with cold martinis.

Soul Speak

Heartbreak. We've all been there. I feel it is safe to say that many have had their hearts broken by someone they love. Many have experienced unrequited love, and many have felt the betrayal and dismay of a lover cheating on them. And many have felt the pain of deep loss when friendships with people they love dissolve or disappear.

If you've never had your heart broken, feel free to bypass this chapter, but if you have, this chapter is for you.

I'm old school. I entered this thing we call life in the city of Cleveland, Ohio, in the year 1960. I came upon Earth during the time when one might have heard the phrase, "That brother is clean," meaning, "That's a well-dressed, good-looking Black Man," or, "That cat sure can play," meaning, "That man is a good musician."

It was a time when men wore hats, women wore heels, and both men and women wore classic, timeless suits. And while not everyone wants to return to wearing stiff shirts, button-up collars, heels, and pearls, it was a time of classic style. At times—and please forgive me for saying this—I feel our present-day fashion pales in comparison to those times. For you see, at the time of this writing, I am nearing my sixtieth birthday, a number that gives me pause when I see it and causes me to become nostalgic.

I was too young to spend much time in the dark, smoky rooms of jazz clubs, but their magic permeated my home through stereophonic music. And for just a few years before the era ended for good, I did experience some of those clubs.

If your heart longs for those times and would like to touch this era cinematically, I highly recommend the classic movie *Paris Blues*, starring Paul Newman, Sidney Poitier, Diahann Carroll, and Joanne Woodward. The film is an achievement in black-and-white cinematography. It is a love story, literally and figuratively. It completely captures the mood and era of the songs and the time, and the era of Nancy Wilson.

"Guess Who I Saw Today" ~ Why I Chose This Song for Goddess Nancy Wilson

If you listen to the words of "Guess Who I Saw Today" and you've suffered heartbreak, you understand what Nancy Wilson is saying. You get it. You understand the story she is telling. She always considered herself a storyteller. In this song, her voice paints the trauma so clearly, you feel the pain. It's a shock when you discover someone you love has cheated on you. It's a shock when you realize you are no longer in love with someone, or sadly they are no longer in love with you. And even though you may find the courage to move on and love again, the memories of those heartbreaks and heartaches can linger in your soul for a long time.

Heartbreak and heartache also don't have to come from romantic relationships. People can get their hearts broken by friends, colleagues, and acquaintances. The breakup of platonic relationships can be just as painful as the breakup of a romantic relationship. How many of us have cried huge tears because we had a fight with a dear friend, or someone we trusted became untrusted and betrayed us? All those things can rip holes in your soul and make you wary of reaching out and becoming vulnerable. And if you have enough of those experiences, bitterness and rotten feelings can take root in places where they can be hard to remove. Hearts are fragile things. Their capacity for love is limitless, but their capacity to scar is not limited to passions of romance. A scarred heart is not easily mended. If your heart has a lot of scar tissue, it can be hard to recover from those wounds.

Not to mention, in this world of social media, you can get your heart broken in tiny ways many times a day. People don't realize how cruel words, texts, or posts can be, and the ability to remain anonymous or use fake accounts allows people to commit all manner of cruel acts upon the hearts of others. The constant barrage has also brought an insensitivity we keep trying to normalize. Personally, I believe this insensitivity is dangerous territory. Not everyone has the healthy boundaries or compassion to navigate the nonstop wheel of expression. Social media has brought weird expectations into our lives. This new world has certainly wrecked the sensitive hearts of many.

The day I found out Nancy Wilson had died, I listened to this song over and over again, and I cried and cried. Crying is cathartic. Some of us cry easier than others. Some of us cry when no one is looking. It doesn't matter. Tears have a purpose. When your heart aches, let the tears flow.

This song by Nancy Wilson pulls the tears out. You can sit and cry with her in the darkness of the café she sings about in her song. There is something so haunting about this song and her voice. On the day of her death, I cried deep tears. I knew in my heart someone great had left us.

Perhaps this may be a song for you, too, if you are heartbroken, grieving, and lamenting a love, a friendship, or a relationship that didn't turn out just right.

I've been married to my true love for more than twenty years and have grown kids and grandchildren—but I have also experienced heartaches and heartbreaks.

Some of us, after having our hearts broken, may choose never to enter love or relationships again. We may feel it's just not worth it. We may feel safer by being alone or not trusting people again with our feelings and emotions. I am not here to judge your decisions when your heart is broken. I *am* here to offer you solace and comfort when you feel sad and alone after someone breaks your heart.

As Nancy tells us in her song, when she realizes what is going on, she chooses to get up and leave. We know tears are in her eyes. We don't know where she goes or what she does after she leaves the bar, but I get the feeling she doesn't go home to wallow in her cornflakes or give up on life. Oh, no; I get the feeling she opens a can of whoop-ass and makes the necessary changes she needs to, to carry on.

So, when you are brokenhearted by love, platonic or romantic, listen to this song by Nancy Wilson. If martinis are your thing, have one (my personal favorite is a dirty gin martini, straight up, made with Tanqueray gin and olives). If martinis aren't for you, pour yourself your favorite libation and settle in for healing time and reflection.

Drown Your Sorrows for Broken Hearts and Promises Ritual

When your heart is broken, you're not in the mood to spend a lot of time on magick. What you need is *healing*.

Items Needed

Your favorite martini or libation

A bowl of water

Florida Water

Rose petals

A small bundle of twigs or sticks

A small box or package of tissues

Small 4-inch red taper candle

Flameproof taper candleholder

Nancy Wilson's song "Guess Who I Saw Today"

Timing

Whenever you feel brokenhearted.

Ritual

Find yourself a comfortable place to sit. Gather all your items. Pour your martini or favorite libation. Place your bowl of water, the Florida Water, the rose petals, the small bundle of twigs or sticks, your box of tissues, and the red candle in its candleholder in front of you.

One of the reasons spell work is powerful is because it works the principle of sympathetic magick. Sympathetic magick is when the items you use in your spells are a stand-in or representation for your feelings associated with the situation for your spell. In this ritual, we are using the twigs to make a sound of breaking—the sound of your heartache over the love that has caused you pain.

Cleanse your red taper candle with the Florida Water.

Listen to "Guess Who I Saw Today" by Nancy Wilson. Take a sip of your libation. Pour some Florida Water into your bowl of water. Notice the scent. Take time to be with the cleansing scent of Florida Water as it wafts from your bowl.

Next, light your red candle. Take a moment to gaze into the flame. As you gaze into the candle flame, slowly pick up a twig and snap it. Continue snapping twigs until you feel a sense of relief. Lay the broken twigs in a pile at the base of your red candle.

Pick up a handful of rose petals. Crush them in your hand and slowly let them fall upon your pile of twigs.

Pick up your pile of broken twigs and crushed rose petals. Slowly allow them to fall into your bowl of water. As the twigs and rose petals fall into the water, think upon your heartache. Allow your feelings to well up and pour out. You may feel anger and sadness. Your feelings are valid. You may need a tissue or two. Take as long as you need. Allow the red candle to burn completely out.

When your candle has completely burned out, take your bowl of water filled with twigs and crushed rose petals and pour the entire mess in the street! Feel relief surge when your mess hits the asphalt or dirt. Don't worry about cleaning it up. Allow Spirit or Mother Nature to get rid of it. Trust you have done your job.

Feel free to repeat this ritual as many times as necessary.

May your heart be soothed and your tears eased.

Creating a Sacred Space for Nancy Wilson

Nancy Wilson was not only known for her legendary voice, but also for her activism. During her lifetime, she received many honors, including the NAACP Image Award and the Jazz Masters Fellowship Award from the National Endowment of the Arts.

In honor of her achievements, find a charitable organization that is committed to the betterment of humanity, the planet, or the environment, and either volunteer with them or make a financial contribution that fits your budget. Our time and our dollars truly can make a difference in this world.

If your city or town has a shop or a store that specializes in the reselling of old vinyl records, plan to visit them. Have fun perusing the stacks. Maybe the vinyl gods will smile upon you, and you'll come across a Nancy Wilson record. If so, and if your budget will allow it, purchase the record and take it to a quiet café or bar. Have your favorite libation or martini. Spend some time looking at the cover. Take out the record and read the liner notes, if there are any. You may be surprised at what you learn. When you get home, put your record somewhere to remind you of the strength and legacy of Nancy Wilson.

eleven
iNCReasiNG pROspeRitY
with abuNdantia

Song: "Forget Me Nots"
Artist: Patrice Rushen

THE GODDESS ABUNDANTIA IS known as a lesser goddess in the Roman pantheon. As such, very little is known about her. However, we do know from online research that "she was a minor Roman goddess who was believed to enter homes during the night to bring prosperity to inhabitants. She was the guardian of the cornucopia, the horn of plenty, from which she distributed food and money. Her name is derived from the Latin word *abundantis*, meaning 'to overflow; to have in large measure'" ("Abundantia").

Hopefully most of us know our democratic society was built upon the foundations of Roman civilization, so who better to honor as a powerful badass goddess than Goddess Abundantia! During Roman times, her face was a symbol upon their golden coins. These coins are so valuable that you could pay more than a pretty penny to own one! I know this because I was blessed to find one at an antique show. Although her coin was out of my price range that day, I keep faith that one day I can own one!

Through her minted image from ancient times, we are called to remember female deities whom societies and civilizations deemed worthy of gracing their currency. And though Abundantia is not the only woman to grace currency, at the time of this writing, those of us living in the United States still await the face of a woman upon paper currency.

Soul Speak

We seek to connect with the Goddess Abundantia to increase our prosperity and abundance frequently and consistently. Since we are seeking to *communicate* with Abundantia, who is benevolent in her graciousness of bestowing prosperity and abundance, I suggest Wednesdays as good days to communicate your wishes to her.

Here's the thing. I'm a Gemini. My ruling planet is *Mercury*. Not only do I keep Mercury oil on my desk, according to *Llewellyn's Witches' Datebook*'s appendix, Wednesdays are associated with the planet Mercury. Combining the power of the planet Mercury, which is associated with communication, makes Wednesdays powerful days of communication for me. I always envision the wings of Mercury speeding my wishes to Goddess Abundantia. So, I do my best, once per waxing moon cycle, on a Wednesday, to work my prosperity altar. However, if you have a day of the week that is better aligned with you, astrologically speaking, then by all means, please use that day!

To communicate with Abundantia means working rites of prosperity several times a year during the cycle of the waxing moon and during astrological occurrences, such as Mercury retrogrades. Case in point, I wrote this piece during a Mercury retrograde. For those unfamiliar, a Mercury retrograde is when the planet Mercury appears to move backward in the sky, thus inflicting all manner of misconstrued havoc on communications, plans, and life itself. As soon as a Mercury retrograde approaches on the calendar, social media begins to blow up with all manner of spells and rituals to combat its destructive influence.

According to *Llewellyn's Moon Sign Datebook*, there are at least three Mercury retrogrades in a year, which I know throws people into a panic around issues of finances. However, if I stopped working my money altar every time there was a Mercury retrograde, I'd be blowin' a hole in all the good juju built over many years of sincere and consistent work.

Sure, it's good to pay attention to signs and astrological occurrences—and if life calls you to be involved in financial matters during a Mercury retrograde, you probably do want to pay special attention to details—but don't let anxiety stop you from doing what you need to do. You've got to work your powerful juju when you need it, and we all need money. Green money, hard cold cash, income. We need money to live, move, and be in this world. Money is the currency of life in these times. It is the tangible exchange of give and receive. "Show me the money!"

Many things have been used as currency in the lifetimes of human beings on Earth: salt, beads, chickens, cows, and countless ways of bartering. We even have "digital dollars" in Bitcoin, PayPal, Venmo, Apple Pay. The list goes on and on. And, of course, there are credit cards. Credit cards can be a dangerous, slippery slope if you don't respect them and know how to use them.

We all need the currency of exchange to get what we need and live life comfortably. Nobody wants or likes to live in poverty. Not having what you need, not being able to afford food, gas, or shelter, is terrible. In my humble opinion, scarcity does not bring you closer to your Higher Power. When you're hungry or cold or can't put gas in your car so you can get to your job, it's awful, and there is no glory in it. And while we're at it, let's drop those vows of poverty we may have taken as spiritual beings. It's okay to get paid and charge for your services! If you don't value yourself financially, how the hell is anyone else going to?

I spent many years climbing the corporate ladder of success. If there was a higher rung, I reached for it. I suppose you could say I have a driven personality. However, everyone's idea of success is different. Not everyone wants to be the boss, CEO, head wizard, high priestess, or grand pooh-bah of their organization. Many have no desire to be in the spotlight or sit at the head of the table. We're all entitled to our own visions, dreams, wishes, and desires.

But what we do share is the need for positive flow, currency, and energetic compensation for the work we do. Every person is deserving of a decent salary, a comfortable place to lay their head, and shelter from the storm.

So let us use powerful juju to effect positive change in our lives and bring about health, wealth, prosperity, and abundance.

"Forget Me Nots" ~ Why I Chose This Song for Goddess Abundantia

The forget-me-not flower *(Myosotis scorpioides)* is a blue flower with a bright yellow center. Its five petals open like sunshine, spreading joy and good feelings whenever you gaze upon them.

Forget-me-not flowers grow in abundance. They love shady, woody places, and they are a perennial-biennial flower, meaning they return every year or every two years. Either way, it is a flower that will grace your garden for many years to come with little or no effort on your part (except for watering and weeding).

This little flower shows forth in all its goodness, mirroring the blue sky and the power of the sun. And surely when abundance flows into our lives, we feel sunny and uplifted. Our cares are lessened, we are hopeful, and the relief from worry gives us opportunities to dream big dreams. We can set our inner sights upon things we would like to achieve for ourselves or manifest into reality for those we hold close to our hearts, for it is hard to dream big dreams when you're scrounging for money, digging in your couch for change so you can fill your gas tank, or living in fear of phone calls from collection agencies. Yet it is exactly during these times we need powerful juju, rites, and rituals to help us out of those dire circumstances.

It's easy to forget who we are, our power, and our magick when it feels like the world is hell-bent on grinding you down, when for every two steps forward, you take seven steps back. And if you're not already feeling bad enough, social media comes along with its world of illusion that everyone is doing so much better *than you*. But wait, there's hope!

This song by Patrice Rushen can help us remember our truth and inspire us to flourish and grow despite hard times. We matter. We can achieve that which we desire if we plant the flower of hope, courage, and strength and tend to it with love and devotion.

The bright spirit of Patrice Rushen lit up my life in the 1980s. I have always found her voice uplifting and refreshing. I love looking at her beautiful face and her gorgeous, long locs (we refer to our hair as "locs" instead of using the word *dreadlock*—there is nothing dreadful about African American hair!) filled with shells on her album covers. She wore her hair that way long before it was trendy. Her smile is so bright, just like the sun. Her music, her songs, and her spirit have definitely lit up my life during dark times. And long, long ago, when I worked at a record store in Boulder, Colorado, I loved placing her album cover up high, where everyone could see and feel her energy as I played her hit songs.

The song "Forget Me Nots" reaches into our consciousness and sends a shaft of light into dark places. Many times, when we're working rites of prosperity, it is because we are in situations of lack. The "lack" subconscious can wreak havoc on our lives. If we constantly see ourselves as lacking or unworthy, it can be hard to visualize ourselves as prosperous and abundant. When we combine Patrice Rushen's voice with rites to Goddess Abundantia, we give ourselves a spiritual lift. And if we do these rites on a consistent basis, we not only get a lift, but we also begin to build a prosperous foundation to stand upon.

It is upon this foundation of prosperity the Romans worshiped Abundantia. She whose image graced their coins, alongside her overflowing cornucopia of abundance.

Flowers Flourish and Coins Everywhere Ritual

During the waxing moon cycle (the cycle from new moon to full moon), gather your items for your ritual. Pick a day when you can perform this ritual between sunrise and noon. We want the power of the growing sunlight and daylight to shine upon your work.

Items Needed

Green cloth to cover your working surface

Florida Water

Green candle (a taper candle or a glass-encased Novena candle)

Cornucopia basket (easily found in craft supply stores)

Coins in several different denominations and, if possible, a
coin with a female face (easily obtained at coin shops
and banks)

Green permanent marker

Petition paper

Olive oil or a blessing oil

White thread knotted 9 times

Fireproof candleholder

Fresh flowers

Timing

Between sunrise and noon, preferably when the time on the
clock is moving from the half hour to the hour (from thirty to
sixty minutes). This is known as the time of increase.

Ritual

Lay down your green cloth.

Using your Florida Water, cleanse your green candle, your
cornucopia basket, and your coins. If you are using a glass-
encased Novena candle, now is the time to use your trusty
green permanent marker. Use your marker to write words,
phrases, or names of loved ones on your candle. Sometimes
I write the word *prosperity* on my candle, and other times I
might write "$$$." Sometimes I include names of family
members on the candle. Use your imagination and intuition
to choose words to write on the glass of your green candle.

Upon your petition paper, write a sincere prayer to the Goddess Abundantia. Tell her your desires for prosperity, health, wealth, and abundance. When you are finished, anoint your paper with olive oil or a blessing oil of your choice in a five-spot pattern. A five-spot pattern is made by placing a drop of oil in all four corners of the paper in a clockwise manner, ending with a drop of oil in the center.

When you have finished anointing your paper, fold the paper until you have a small packet. Make the first fold toward yourself. This symbolizes bringing blessings *to you*. Tie your packet with your white thread and set it aside.

Anoint your green candle with your blessing oil. Place it in a fireproof candleholder and light the wick. If you are using a glass-encased candle, light the wick.

Place your petition paper inside the cornucopia. Fill your cornucopia with coins so that some of them spill onto your working surface. Lay your fresh flowers around the cornucopia.

Close your eyes and envision your life filled with all you desire and that which you have written upon your petition paper. Thank the Goddess Abundantia for hearing your prayers.

You can allow your taper candle to burn safely down or pinch it out and save it for the next time you do the ritual. If you are using a glass-encased Novena candle, you can allow the candle to burn until a clear pool of wax has formed. Then, snuff or pinch out the flame and save the candle for the next time you perform the ritual.

●●●●●●●●●●●●●●●●●●

Creating a Sacred Space for Abundantia

After you have completed your ritual for the Goddess Abundantia, you may want to connect with her on a regular basis, outside of the ritual described. Creating a sacred altar space for the goddess you have called upon to aid you is a lovely, magickal way to keep her powerful presence in your life. You can leave the altar up for as long as you deem necessary. You can also create this sacred space without performing the ritual described; however, you will find the sacred space more meaningful once you have the called upon the goddess to aid you in your troubles.

Items Needed

Cornucopia

Petition paper

Coins, green cloth, blessing oil

Florida Water

A green taper candle

Plastic wrap

Golden glitter

Fireproof candleholder

To create your sacred space for Goddess Abundantia, use the cornucopia filled with your petition paper, your coins, your green cloth, and your blessing oil. You can also use a condition oil for prosperity, which can easily be obtained online or in metaphysical supply stores.

Pick a space where you can set up your items and they will not be disturbed. If it is not safe for you to create a permanent space (you don't want naysayers or nonbelievers throwing their negative energy upon your work), you can keep all your items in a lovely box of your choosing and take them out to work with them once a month. When you are finished, you can place everything back in the box and place the box in a safe space.

Once you have gathered all your items and decided upon a space or box, during a waxing moon cycle (from new moon to full moon, which is a spiritual time of increase), anoint your sacred space with Florida Water and cover it with the green cloth. Cleanse your green candle with the Florida Water. Upon the green candle, carve any words that connote success or prosperity to you.

Lay down your plastic wrap. This makes for an easy cleanup.

Anoint the candle with your blessing or prosperity oil. Sprinkle golden glitter over your candle and place the candle in the fireproof candleholder.

Place the candle and the cornucopia filled with your petition paper and coins upon the green cloth.

Light your candle.

Say a sincere prayer of thanksgiving and gratitude for all the blessings you have received and for all the blessings that are on their way to you, *right now.* This is a confirmation of your faith, your belief, that good things are on their way to you!

Allow your candle to safely burn all the way out. If that isn't possible, pinch or snuff it out, and save it for the time you enter into your sacred space with Goddess Abundantia.

Spend time with Goddess Abundantia in your sacred space. If you will be keeping your altar set up, choose a place where you can pass it daily to remind you of the good work you have done to bring your goals, dreams, wishes, and desires into manifestation. Also, you can add any items that find their way to you that symbolize success, prosperity, and manifestation. Once you start working with Abundantia, you'll be amazed at the trinkets, papers, and whatnots that will find their way to you, all telling you she is with you, blessing you with her cornucopia of abundance, which is limitless and always flowing, pouring goodness over you.

You may also wonder how you will know if your prosperity juju is working. While we all love to believe in the golden coins that seem to pour forth from the end of the rainbow, successful prosperity work shows in small ways over the long haul. Sure, it's fantastic to get an unexpected windfall in the mail or a check for hundreds of dollars you weren't expecting (wouldn't we all love that), but the work you are doing is to increase your *prosperity*. I like the word *prosperity* because it covers a larger range of blessings than simply a check in the mail.

As you consistently work your prosperity magick over time, putting in sincere effort along with your prayers of thanksgiving to the Goddess Abundantia, what may start to happen (as I have experienced it) is your prosperity increases in various and wonderful ways.

For example, here are some things that have created prosperity in my life as I continue to work my prosperity magick:

- My tax refund showed up earlier than expected.
- A medical bill was reduced, and I owed less money than I had anticipated.
- I was given a stipend as a bonus for work I was doing.
- A family member got a new job with a significant raise.
- A conference offered to pay for my travel, lodgings, and expenses.

All these things translate to prosperity and what I call spiritual financial credits. Some credits are actual cold, hard cash, while others allow me to move more comfortably in the world and experience things I might not have been able to experience without these gifts.

These things contribute to your financial ease of mind and the flow of prosperity in your life. So, when you work with the Goddess Abundantia, be sure not to put any limitations around what you perceive to be financial blessings. Her blessings can show up in a myriad of ways for you and for your family, friends, and loved ones. Allow yourself to stay open to the flow of positive, powerful juju you have invoked into your life!

twelve
self-reflection and insight through sybil leek

Song: "Time after Time"
Artist: Cyndi Lauper

SYBIL LEEK WAS BORN on February 22, 1917, in Stoke-on-Trent, Staffordshire, England. She came from the old country of Witches: New Forest, Britain. She was a powerful trance medium, teacher, lecturer, and author. She participated in parapsychological investigations, also known as ghost hunting.

Her psychic vision was powerful. As a child she could "see" things about people, and more than once, she said things that unnerved them. When she participated in ghost hunting adventures or in séances, she would go into such a deep trance she couldn't remember anything she said, and the experiences would leave her drained.

She had to learn to take care of herself and pace herself through all the demands put upon her.

Although she was famous, first and foremost, she was a Witch. She was candid about being a Witch and spoke openly about her Craft. She knew Aleister Crowley when she was a child, as he liked to drop by and visit the home where she lived with her family and her grandmother. She was one of the first people to "come out of the broom closet" after the laws against Witchcraft were repealed in the 1950s in England. Through her books, interviews, and articles, she has left a legacy for us to return to time after time.

Sybil Leek was a true medium and didn't use tarot cards in her readings. She also wasn't a fan of crystal balls or dark curtains used to create ambiance in a session, but she did see the value in people coming to the world of the Occult through these practices. You have to remember, Sybil Leek came to America in the 1960s, and so many things we take for granted now were just beginning to emerge and become popular and accessible.

Sybil Leek was highly educated due to coming from a strong hereditary line of Witches and through her own gifts. She believed in reincarnation. She also gave countless interviews, authored sixty books, was a newspaper reporter, owned an antique shop in England, and had a famous jackdaw who sat on her shoulder. She was initiated into a coven in England and appeared on TV shows, all as a Witch! She never cowered from the title or separated who she was or what she did from being a Witch. She was proud of it! That is quite a feat for a woman living during those times. If you are reading this and considering whether or not to call yourself a Witch, remember those who have gone before you and the shoulders you stand upon.

Although Sybil was proud, she was never arrogant. She simply was. And that is the bravery I see in her. She stood up for her beliefs. She lived them and expressed them. Sure, there were detractors, cynics, and skeptics, but through her reputation and steadfastness, no one could deny who she was. And it is for that reason I have included her in this book. We all need women to look to for inspiration and guidance. She was a brave soul. She left the earth plane on October 26, 1982, and her ashes were taken to Dorset, England, for interment.

Soul Speak

I never met Sybil Leek or knew her personally. She had lived a tremendous life and had already passed from the land of the living by the time I came to know about her. However, during my research, I did get a kick from discovering that, for a brief moment in history, she and I shared a physical space in geography. When she lived in Los Angeles, California, I was a child living in Los Angeles at the same time!

Her Witchy influence must have flown over me somehow, because I do give credit to growing up in LA during the '60s and '70s for putting a spell on me that has never left. During those times, music was filled with songs about spells and magic. There were flower children and hippies, and the magical muse was strong. I loved my chokers, hot pants, and time spent roaming Hollywood and going to the beach with my cousins.

One of my favorite things about her was how she stood up for Witches. She spoke so eloquently about how we love nature and our "zest" for living (Leek 1968, 151). She also considered herself an eternal optimist, yet she knew the struggle and the loneliness that occur as a person goes further and deeper into learning about the Occult and its practices. She knew how lonely it can be for someone who is a true and sincere seeker to walk the path of alternative religions, and she practiced her Craft as a religion. She referred to it as the Old Religion. For her, it was a way of life, which included a belief in a Supreme Being and sidestepping the pitfalls of darkness, which can occur when magickal people lose their way, seduced by lure of power and Occult knowledge. There is truth in the phrase "with great power comes great responsibility."

Sybil Leek knew about self-defensive magick. During my research, I came across information stating she "cursed" people. I don't know if any of that is true, but I do know the word *curse* gives people the willies.

It has always been my intent to portray Witches and the Craft in a positive light. I learned Sybil Leek felt the same way. However, this is a book about powerful juju for troubled times. We do need to know how to use our Craft to protect and defend ourselves and our loved ones, should the need arise. And this is where I draw a line.

Just as martial arts are the practice of self-defense, so should self-defensive magick follow the same ethics. Bragging about what you can and will do to someone as a Witch, Occultist, practitioner, conjurer, or whatever a person chooses to call themselves in the magickal realm is a form of bullying. Doing so may bring painful lessons into your life. If a person chooses to promote themselves as such, I stay clear away from them. A hint to the wise is sufficient.

So let us embrace the powerful legacy of Sybil Leek for guidance and assistance when the troubled times come upon us.

"Time after Time" ~ Why I Chose This Song for Goddess Sybil Leek

When I hear Cyndi Lauper sing "Time after Time," I can't help but think of Sybil Leek. There is something ethereal and mystical in the great Cyndi Lauper's voice that brings me closer to the spirit of Sybil Leek. I have been charmed by Sybil's autobiography, *Diary of a Witch*, her immense legacy, and her transcendent power as a medium. At times, it feels as if she is very close to me, spurring me on in my own unique expression as a Witch. And as someone who was a prolific published writer, she inspires me to carry on with my own writing.

Witch is a powerful word. It speaks to the strength and power of women and men who are deeply attuned to nature, the seasons, the turn of the wheel of life, the Occult, and those who seriously study their Craft. Being a Witch is a lifetime commitment. Witchcraft is a practice. It is a living, breathing art that continues to grow and evolve, as long you claim it and make it so. It is limitless and unbounded. You can learn things about the Craft, use them, and improve upon them for your entire lifetime.

When you search for an image of Sybil Leek, you will immediately see she doesn't fit the stereotypical image of a Witch. From the cover of her autobiography, *Diary of a Witch*, Sybil Leek's eyes stare up into our eyes. She is wearing dark eyeliner, and it appears she is holding a necklace. She has a round face, and it looks like she has a gap between her front two teeth. She's an older woman in this photo, and her hair and clothing are stylish. Her smile is welcoming and engaging. I can imagine sharing a cup of tea with her and chatting about Witchcraft through long afternoon shadows.

"Time after Time" has a haunting, long-lasting, forever quality to it. I've listened to it so many times since it was first released that I've lost count. Not only does it touch my heart as a song, but it was also featured in one of my favorite movies, *Strictly Ballroom*. While that has nothing to do with Sybil Leek, it is a magickal touchstone for me. If you're looking for a feel-good classic and you're a fan of ballroom dancing, do yourself a favor and check out that movie.

Sybil Leek was such a strong believer in reincarnation, ghosts, spirits, and the world of the unseen, I feel in my heart that after her spirit left her physical body, she just kept going. Through her strong family upbringing in Britain and her own personal beliefs, she stated in her autobiography that she didn't fear death. From her perspective, she believed when death comes to the physical body, it simply means the soul has learned all it needs to know in this adventure. It's time for a new adventure. It's time to move on.

●●●●●●●●●●●●●●●●●●●●

Mirror, Mirror Ritual

Sybil Leek was a famous psychic medium. She was internationally famous for her ability to go into a trance and commune with spirits and ghosts; however, she never went about conjuring up spirits to "work for her." She simply communicated with them to help others.

For this ritual, we are going to communicate with ourselves from a higher plane. Most of the rituals I've written in this book are to help navigate troubled waters and provide healing. But there is also the need to defend yourself, especially if you are empathetic or sensitive or if you are public about your Occult practices or "alternative religious" ways.

Items Needed

White candle

Florida Water

A mirror

Soft white cloth

Salt

Bowl of water

Flameproof candleholder

Darkened room

Timing

Whenever you feel the need for self-reflection and healing.

Ritual

Cleanse your white candle with Florida Water and set it aside.

Cleanse your mirror with Florida Water. To cleanse your mirror, anoint the mirror in a five-spot pattern. A five-spot pattern is when you place a drop of Florida Water in a corner of the mirror and continue clockwise, adding a drop to all four corners and finishing with a dab of Florida Water in the center of the mirror.

Once you've finished anointing the mirror, allow it to dry. Once the water is dry, blow your breath over the glass and wipe the mirror with the soft white cloth until the mirror is shiny and clean.

Next, gather your salt and your bowl of water. Cup the bowl of water between your hands and say,

Blessed be element of water.

Pour a bit of salt into your palm and say,

Blessed be element of earth.

Add three pinches of salt to the bowl of water.

Pour a small amount of Florida Water into the bowl of salted water.

Place your white candle in the flameproof candleholder. Place the mirror so you can see your reflection. Place the bowl of scented, salted water in front of the mirror. Darken your room by closing the curtains or blinds or by dimming the lights.

Light your candle.

Take a deep breath.

Slowly and lightly breathe in through your nose and out through your mouth, gently, so as to not extinguish your candle flame.

Gently breathe in through your nose and out through your mouth until you feel relaxed.

Once you are relaxed, pick up your candle. Hold the candle so you can see the flame and your reflection in the mirror. Say,

I am a light that shines bright. Though shadows
follow me, I keep to the light. I acknowledge darkness
is part of me, as night follows day. I give thanks for
the pitfalls along my way. I heal, love, and forgive
myself for things I may have said or done. I arise
from this darkness and walk in the Sun.

Pinch out your candle. Cover your mirror with your soft cloth.

Place your candle and mirror in a safe place where you can use them again when you feel the need to repeat this ritual. Dispose of your scented, salted water by pouring it down your sink or in the street in front of your home.

●●●●●●●●●●●●●●●●●●

Creating a Sacred Space for Sybil Leek

After you have completed your ritual for the Goddess Sybil Leek, you may want to connect with her on a regular basis, outside of the ritual described. Creating a sacred altar space for the goddess you have called upon to aid you is a lovely, magickal way to keep her powerful presence in your life. You can leave the altar up for as long as you deem necessary. You can also create this sacred space without performing the ritual described; however, you will find the sacred space more meaningful once you have the called upon the goddess to aid you in your troubles.

Items Needed

A black cloth

A white candle

Florida Water

Flameproof candleholder

An image of a jackdaw or a faux blackbird

A small libation (drink of your choice)

A small cracker, piece of bread, or piece of cake

A small plate

Greenery (wreath or spray of real or faux flowers)

Timing

In this day and age, Witchcraft is a hot topic. Social media abounds with hashtags and private and public groups for people who align or associate with the word *Witch*. There are even Witch wars and drama in online forums, where people berate each other over what is the true meaning of being a Witch or what constitutes a real Witchcraft practice.

As I have previously shared, Sybil Leek was one of the first Witches to have a public persona. She gave countless interviews and appeared on many television shows. By creating this sacred space for her through the form of a powerful ritual, we can tap into the self-defensive and strong boundaries she had as an "out of the broom closet" Witch, to sustain ourselves as Witches, or as people who choose to be public about our magickal practices.

Prepare yourself to have all your items ready by the time of 11:15 p.m. on October 31. Make sure you will not be disturbed.

As one would imagine, the Sabbat of Samhain (as we now call it), or the time of Halloween, was important to Sybil. In her autobiography, she wrote about having to sneak out to the woods with the assistance of her family so she could attend the Sabbat without being seen or tracked by curiosity seekers who were on a "Witch hunt." Can you imagine the dedication, planning, tenacity, and commitment it took for her to do that?! Yet she did it. She was successful in reaching the secret meeting place and was able to complete her rites, which finished at 3:00 a.m.

So, for our sacred space for Sybil Leek, we will create a space that goes up during Samhain or Halloween and then is removed when that holiday has passed.

Ritual

Gather all your items.

Lay your black cloth on a flat surface.

Cleanse your candle with Florida Water. The act of cleansing your candle sets the tone that you are entering a magickal space and purifies your candle from others who may have touched it prior to you using it for your rite.

Place the white candle in the flameproof candleholder. Set the candle in the center of the black cloth.

Place your faux blackbird or jackdaw image on the black cloth.

Place your libation and cracker, cake, or bread upon the small plate.

Form a circle around the bird and the candle with your greenery. Be sure the circle is wide enough to enclose the bird and the candle, yet far enough away so the candle will burn safely.

When the hour strikes midnight, light your candle.

Say,

> *Dear Sybil, upon this hour on this sacred night, we honor you in love and light. Thank you for your courage, bravery, and brilliance. Thank you for showing us a way to connect with the Craft. Thank you for your blessing of protection as we seek to move forward as Witches. May your spirit always be lively, happy, and bright.*

Break off a piece of your cracker, cake, or bread, and set it aside on the small plate. Raise your cup, which holds your drink, and pour a small amount of your libation upon your cracker, cake, or bread. Thank the Divine Mother Earth for always providing you with all you need.

Now, eat the rest of your food and finish your drink as you sit with your burning candle in this sacred space for as long as you feel called to. Think upon all those who have been persecuted as Witches. Think about what the word *Witch* means to you. Think upon the bravery and courage of women in this day and age who stand up for their beliefs.

When you are finished, place all your items in a safe place that you designate as sacred for Sybil Leek. Whenever you see a crow fly by, silently acknowledge it as a magickal creature and remember Sybil Leek's jackdaw, who was her familiar and so important to her practice.

thirteen
Help Carrying On
from doreen valiente

Song: "Chasing Pavements"
Artist: Adele

DOREEN WAS BORN ON January 4, 1922, in Colliers Wood, Mitcham, Surrey, England. By all appearances, she was a "normal" woman, though she was almost six feet tall! She didn't walk around in Witchy garb or flashy clothing. For all her superpowers, she was a woman you may have passed in the grocery store without ever knowing who you were walking next to.

Doreen Valiente was a stalwart person. She lived during World War II and worked as a civil servant. During this time, she worked on classified documents, serving her country while continuing with her passion for Witchcraft.

She didn't live an extravagant life. She lived in simple flats, yet she was blessed with an overflowing wealth of knowledge and spirituality from the unseen spirits of the Occult and the Craft, to whom she dedicated her life as a Witch. Her "The Charge of the Goddess" remains the most popular piece of liturgy in the world of the Craft today.

Doreen Valiente was an author, a poet, and a lifelong student of the Occult, and she was initiated by Gerald Gardner. Although she might not have agreed with me calling her a goddess, she is one in my mind, through her ability to effect and bring about positive change and her willingness to impart knowledge and wisdom that spans across time. She is clearly a woman deserving of recognition, respect, and honor.

Doreen was undeterred in her quest for seeking knowledge and truth. No one told her to do it. She just did it. She followed her hunches, wrote newspaper articles, and sought out like-minded others to form groups and covens and to bring the Craft—or Wicca, as it is called today—into being.

No matter what we call it today, Doreen Valiente was first and foremost a Witch. She was a prolific writer, and her words spur the heart and call us forth in the darkest of moments. She lived during a time when the laws against Witchcraft had just been repealed, making it easier to contact other seekers. And though it may be hard to believe those laws were only repealed in the 1950s in Britain, many of the practices, rites, and rituals we ascribe to today are less than one hundred years old.

But none of that really matters, for when you read about Doreen Valiente and what she truly believed and wanted, I feel she would be pleased to know so many in this day refer to themselves as Witches and are out of the broom closet.

She passed away on September 1, 1999. Her ashes were scattered somewhere near or around Sussex, England. In 2013, Britain recognized her life by awarding her home in Tyson Place, Brighton, the highest honor of designation for a historic place: the blue plaque.

Soul Speak

Doreen Valiente's books are some of the most precious on my shelves. I'm particularly partial to my authenticated copy of *Where Witchcraft Lives*, a limited edition of just a thousand gold-stamped and sealed books produced by the Centre for Pagan Studies.

This book will never leave my home, and I will never loan it to anyone. For I never know when or if I shall return to London, and this unique copy can never be duplicated. London is such a special place. One of the things I enjoyed during my two visits there was seeing and standing in places, touching the stones or the earth of mystical or historic sites that one only reads about in books or sees in movies or on TV. If you are a seeker or a practitioner, align with the word *Witch*, or believe in magick, I highly recommend putting traveling to London on your life list of things to accomplish.

Although I never made it to Brighton, which was the last place Doreen lived, and I never met her in person, she holds a deep, special, and abiding place in my heart. When the moon rises, her words, written in "The Charge of the Goddess," resonate in my heart and call to me. While Gerald Gardner is normally credited as the father of modern Witchcraft, it was Doreen Valiente who put those famous words to paper, and it was Doreen who broke away from him when she realized she needed to move on. It was Doreen who quietly and fervently continued to carry the torch for Witches until she died.

When I first set upon the path of Witchcraft, I would hear Doreen's famous words uttered at Pagan gatherings, in rituals, and in ceremonies. Seems everyone knew the words "all acts of love and pleasure are my rituals" (Valiente 2014, 13).

When I got serious about expressing my true Witch nature, I decided I should be able to say the entire "Charge" by memory, and so that is exactly what I set about doing. I copied the entire prose into my book of shadows, and then I set about memorizing it.

On one magickal summer night during a Pagan gathering, in a creek with fireflies gracing the air, I was asked to say "The Charge," and out it came. That night shall always remain one of the most magickal experiences in my life.

From that experience, many other magickal opportunities and gifts followed. But even as I spoke those words and continued to do so every full moon, there was something about the words that just didn't seem right to me. There were gender references in the prose that didn't fit. But I continued to say the words as I had come to them.

As my love and adoration for Doreen continued to grow and blossom, I joined the Doreen Valiente Foundation. The foundation and the Centre for Pagan Studies are dedicated and committed to keeping her legacy and spirit alive. I received a membership certificate and some other goodies, and I also purchased *The Charge of the Goddess: Expanded Edition with New and Previously Unpublished Poems*.

When I received my book, the first thing I did was look up "The Charge of the Goddess." Boy, was I surprised. The very words I had struggled with for so long were not in the text. I also saw paragraphs and words that are routinely omitted when I hear people read or sing "The Charge."

Doreen's original words, written in "The Charge of the Goddess" as she intended them, are inclusive, loving, and powerful. So, I copied the "new" original version into my Book of Shadows, and this is the version I now say when I stand before the full moon.

"The Charge of the Goddess" is the only universal piece of liturgy we as Witches have. Whatever your feelings are about Paganism or Wicca (and for the record, I have never been initiated into the path of Wicca, nor do I refer to myself as Wiccan), I deeply suggest you use "The Charge of the Goddess" published by the Doreen Valiente Foundation. Read and learn her words as she originally intended them.

I am honored to have been granted permission by the Doreen Valiente Foundation to include "The Charge of the Goddess" in the pages of this book. You will find it printed in its entirety in the ritual section.

I also suggest adding to your bookshelf *Doreen Valiente Witch* by Philip Heselton. This phenomenal account of Doreen Valiente's life is a must-have for any person seriously interested in the origins of the Craft. It is also a magnificent, detailed accounting of the life and times of Doreen Valiente and how she came to be our Mother Witch.

"Chasing Pavements" ~ Why I Chose This Song for Goddess Doreen Valiente

Adele. A one-word name. A voice that shakes heaven and Earth. A nobody to a somebody. Loved and adored by millions of people across the planet. Famous for so many songs. So why this song? Why does this song call out to me for Goddess Mother Witch Doreen Valiente?

On YouTube, there is a video of Adele singing this song at the age of twenty: "Adele—'Chasing Pavements' LIVE from the Archive." The footage is in black and white. Adele is accompanied by a young man playing the guitar. It is only her, the young man, and the guitar. Her hair is messy. She's wearing a wool cap, very little makeup or perhaps none at all, and dark clothing. Her voice is raw, clear, and emotional. This video is priceless in that it was recorded before she reached fame and stardom. It is her as a musician, the songstress, in her pure form. And in that moment, she touches our heart with her delivery.

While researching the song "Chasing Pavements," I discovered it was recorded spontaneously by Adele on her phone after she had a bad breakup with a boyfriend. She was heartbroken and recorded the song as she was walking down the street. Later, the song was polished and published.

Adele's ability to simply lay out her feelings in this song, which touched the hearts of millions, describes the effect Doreen Valiente has had on those who practice Witchcraft, call themselves Witches, or practice Wicca. And both women are Brits, hailing from the land from which the roots of Western magick have spread far and wide across the world.

When Adele recorded this song, Doreen had already left the earth plane. Nine years had passed between her death and Adele singing "Chasing Pavements." Surely, on that day when Adele broke up with her boyfriend, who had cheated on her, and poured her heart into her phone, she had no idea the lasting effect it would have on people.

And the same for Doreen Valiente. Surely in her lifetime, she had no idea the effect her work, her presence, her books, her journey, and her life would have on countless people. In fact, toward the end of her life, she gave a presentation at the Centre for Pagan Studies, and she was amazed over two thousand people came to hear her speak. She thought she was going to be in a small room, speaking to a tiny group of people! Such was her humility and not knowing the effect she had on people's lives, especially those of us who are called to the Goddess and feel deeply attuned to the word *Witch*.

Doreen Valiente could have given up. As Adele sings in her song, Doreen could have assumed the work she did in her lifetime was just chasing pavements of the Occult, which might have never led to anything successful, real, or tangible. As many of us know, when we set on the path of the Occult as true seekers and sincere believers, it does seem at times that we're just following sidewalks that lead to nowhere.

The Craft is a mystery. It can never be fully explained; it can only be felt and experienced. You can only know it from within yourself. You can only hold it when you commit to it, when you honor and keep to your rites and practices and acknowledge the moon. When you do this, you touch with all the ancient ones—the ones who have gone before, who stood under the moon and knew its power. Those who honored it and kept to its light in the darkest of times.

Keep Calm and Carry On Ritual

In this ritual, we turn to the strength of the Witch to keep calm and help us carry on. In the spirit of the powerful circle that sustains all who seek to call themselves Witches, the practice and rites of Witchcraft are a powerful way of life. They help us not only when the sun is shining, but when troubled times come. For as much as we love sunshine, it is the power of the moon, shining in the dark, our beacon of hope, that gets us through dark times, storms of the soul, self-doubt, anxiety, and fear of the unknown.

One of the most powerful things about this ritual is that it is done in secret. As a student of the Occult, you will learn many rites and rituals are done in private. Knowledge is only shared with those participating or with those who may be on a "need to know" basis.

Items Needed

Your favorite incense

A fireproof holder for your incense

Salt

A bowl of water

A white candle

Fireproof candleholder

A small, sweet treat (cake, chocolate, candy, bread, or
   cracker)

Your favorite libation

A small plate for your sweet treat

"The Charge of the Goddess" by Doreen Valiente

Timing

You can perform this ritual the night before the full moon, the
night of the full moon, or the night after the full moon.

Ritual

Gather all your items. Choose a time and a place when and
where you will not be disturbed.

Before you begin, take a ritual bath or shower. Wash yourself with intention, as you are about to enter a sacred space.
You can use your favorite soap or bath gel or just plain water.
What matters most is to set your mind, body, and spirit into a
sacred, spiritual groove.

After your bath, put on fresh, clean clothes. I like to wear
my favorite Witchy garb. I have several flowy outfits that work

for this type of ritual. If you choose to perform this ritual outside, you can add layers for warmth. Doreen was known to perform rituals skyclad (naked), covered only by her woolen cloak! If you choose to perform this ritual naked, that is fine, too. It is totally up to you to cover or not to cover yourself. This is your private rite between you and the Goddess Moon.

Once you are clean and ready, take all your items to the place you will perform this ritual.

For this ritual, we are going to cast a circle. Casting a circle forms a protective barrier around yourself as you enter sacred space. We shall cast a circle proper in a way that has become powerful for me—that I can turn to when things get rough and I truly wish to touch with the power of the Goddess as she shines in the night, as the full moon shining bright.

I strongly urge you to read all the directions first and become familiar with the steps before you begin. You can also write out the steps in your own handwriting and use them to help you as you perform this rite.

Casting the Circle

First, cleanse your space with your incense. Light your incense and carry it around the circle in a clockwise manner as the incense is smoking. Say,

Blessed be element of air.

Next, add salt to your water. Cup your bowl of water. Say,

Blessed be element of water. Water
which cleanses, blesses, and refreshes.

Pour a small amount of salt into the palm of your hand. Say,

Blessed be element of earth.

Add three pinches of salt to your bowl of water.

Next, walk your circle and sprinkle salted water all around it. When you have finished sprinkling water, return the bowl of water to its place.

Now you will call upon the powers of the four directions (east, south, west, north) to bless and guard your circle. Face east. Assume the position of the Goddess: stand with your arms raised toward the sky. Say,

Thank you, powers of East,
for being a guard unto my Circle.

Continue making this greeting to the south, west, and north, returning to the east when you are finished. Say,

The Circle is cast! I, [insert your name], do humbly and
graciously call upon the Goddess to be with me in my rite.

Light the white candle. Say,

Blessed be element of fire.

Once the circle has been blessed and guarded, return to the center of the circle with your white candle. Recite "The Charge of the Goddess." After performing this ritual many times, if you are serious about your Craft, challenge yourself to recite "The Charge" from memory.

"The Charge of the Goddess"
by Doreen Valiente

Listen to the words of the Great Mother, who was of old also called Artemis; Astarte; Diana; Melusine; Aphrodite; Cerridwen; Dana; Arianrhod; Isis; Bride; and by many other names.

Whenever ye have need of anything, once in a month, and better it be when the Moon be full, then ye shall assemble in some secret place and adore the spirit of me, who am Queen of all Witcheries.

There shall ye assemble, ye who are fain to learn all sorcery, yet have not yet won its deepest secrets: to these will I teach things that are yet unknown. And ye shall be free from slavery; and as a sign that ye are really free, ye shall be naked in your rites; and ye shall dance, sing, feast, make music and love, all in my praise. For mine is the ecstasy of the spirit and mine also is joy on earth; for my Law is Love unto all Beings.

Keep pure your highest ideal; strive ever toward it; let naught stop you or turn you aside. For mine is the secret door which opens upon the Land of Youth; and mine is the Cup of the

Wine of Life, and the Cauldron of Cerridwen, which is the Holy Grail of Immortality.

I am the Gracious Goddess, who gives the gift of joy unto the heart. Upon earth, I give the knowledge of the spirit eternal; and beyond death, I give peace and freedom, and reunion with those who have gone before. Nor do I demand sacrifice, for behold I am the Mother of All Living, and my love is poured out upon the earth.

Hear ye the words of the Star Goddess, she in the dust of whose feet are the hosts of heaven; whose body encircleth the Universe; I, who am the beauty of the green earth, and the white Moon, among the stars, and the mystery of the waters and the heart's desire, call unto thy soul. Arise and come unto me.

For I am the Soul of Nature, who giveth life to the Universe; from me all things proceed, and unto me must all things return; and before my face, beloved of gods and mortals, thine inmost divine self shall be unfolded in the rapture of infinite joy.

Let my worship be within the heart that rejoiceth, for behold: all acts of love and pleasure are my rituals. And therefore let there be beauty and strength, power and compassion, honour and humility, mirth and reverence within you.

And thou who thinkest to seek for me, know thy seeking and yearning shall avail thee not, unless thou know this mystery: that if that which thou seekest thou findest not within thee, thou wilt never find it without thee.

For behold, I have been with thee from the beginning; and I am that which is attained at the end of desire.

—Doreen Valiente

After you have recited "The Charge," take time to pour out your thoughts, feelings, and emotions to the Goddess. Tell her what ails you, what you need. Ask the Goddess to help you carry on during your times of trouble. This is your opportunity to candidly converse with she of many names who has come to be with you in your circle. It is your moment to weep, cry, rage, scream, and let go of emotions that are affecting your peace and serenity.

You may also choose to say a prayer of protection for your family, friends, and loved ones. Say the names of those who are dear to you, who may need blessings of protection, safety, health, or abundance. Say whatever is on your heart.

When you have finished speaking your truth, offer a piece of your sweet treat and a drink to the Goddess. Set aside a piece of your treat on the small plate. Pour a small amount of your libation upon it as an offering.

Eat the remaining portion of your cake. Drink the remaining portion of your libation. Sit awhile and enjoy the power of your rite.

When you are ready to close the circle, thank the Goddess for being with you. Release the guardians of the four directions, moving in counterclockwise fashion, beginning in the direction of north.

Assume the Goddess position (feet apart and arms raised). Say,

> *Thank you, guardians of the North,*
> *for being a guard unto my Circle.*

Continue thanking each direction until you finish with the direction of east.

Snuff or pinch out your candle if it is still burning. Safely extinguish your incense if it is still burning. Dispose of your libation and cake offering by leaving it outside in your yard or placing it in the earth. You can use a potted plant as your earth receptacle, or you can take your offering to a park and leave it by a tree. Use your imagination. And if none of those options are available to you, simply place your offering outside with a prayer of thanksgiving.

Feel the power and elation of casting a circle and being with the Divine Mother Goddess.

May all be well with you.

Creating a Sacred Space for Doreen Valiente

Doreen Valiente was a lifelong student of the Occult. She had a massive library and a few close friends, but hundreds admired her. She was shy and reclusive, and she never wanted to be worshiped or have a shrine built in her honor.

So, in keeping with her wishes, we won't create a sacred space for her. Instead, we will hold her in our hearts and keep her memory as Mother Witch alive. The things she gave to us through her words, her poems, her writings, and her articles are legendary contributions to Witches all over the world.

We will remember her when we look at the moon and when we recite the powerful words she wrote in "The Charge of the Goddess." We will hold ourselves in high esteem and realize the Craft is a living, breathing art—one that continues to grow, change, and evolve through those who practice it. It is not something meant to be shelved away or portrayed as evil. It is a help, a gift, a blessing, and a guide to those who honor it properly.

After reading these words, if you feel moved to do so, please consider making a contribution to the Doreen Valiente Foundation via the Centre for Pagan Studies, which is dedicated to keeping the legacy and magick of dear Doreen alive.

fourteen
Magickal Inspirations
for Coming Days

THE WORLD HAS FALLEN down several times during the writing of this book. There has been a global pandemic, the deaths of iconic people, horrible murders, wildfires, and countless other stressors that have tested people to their core. There has been disappointment over planned events canceled, loneliness, and fear. Everyone has sought ways to cope, heal, and carry on. And no matter how psychic or magickal we consider ourselves to be, none of us saw the events of 2020 on the horizon.

It can be heartbreaking to see those we love suffering. It can be devastating to our empathic and sympathetic souls to perform these works, only to watch things remain the same. When this happens, we may be tempted to toss our tools, hope, faith, and beliefs right into the trash can. I say this from experience.

Even I, as a magickal spiritual person, have had many doubts. I believe having doubts and questions are signs of normalcy and humility. Even I have questioned if what I was doing was correct or if all I believe is true. More than once I've thrown out magickal tools, ripped down sacred spaces, or stepped away from people, places, and things that I thought were the answer to my problems.

Along with using powerful juju and magickal tools and working your Craft to bring positive change into your life, and perhaps to others, we need to speak about the reality of magick, the power of self-will, and acceptance. No matter how hard we try to change a situation for others, we must accept that we can only truly change ourselves. The old phrase holds true that, even in magick, "you can lead a horse to water, but you can't make it drink."

So, when you've worked your ass off and done all you can to use your powerful juju for troubled times and things still haven't changed, *let go.* Don't beat yourself up about what you may perceive as a failure. For even in dark times when you've done all you can, when you don't see the results you've hoped for, there are still gains and benefits, ripples of good juju you've sent out into the world. They may just take a little while to return to you. Remember that there is always good mixed in with the bad.

A Blessing Received

During the writing of this book, I have received many gifts and blessings. In February 2020, I was chosen to be a fellow in the Sojourner Truth Leadership Circle. The Sojourner Truth Leadership Circle is sponsored and created by Auburn Seminary. Its function is to support and uplift Black Women whom they consider to be the spiritual background of the United States of America.

The fellowship into which I was accepted is the third cohort for this circle, and it is called Healing for Healers. Ironic, isn't it, that this cohort for healers occurred during one of the most trying times in recent human history. This honor was given to twelve Black Women, and honestly, when the email first landed in my inbox, I didn't believe it. I couldn't believe I was being awarded this magnificent opportunity.

In the body of the email were the words, "We see you," along with the motto of Auburn Seminary: "Trouble the waters. Heal the world" (Auburn Seminary).

It was as if someone had peered into my heart and seen the real me. I cried for days. To even have my name mentioned in the same breath as Sojourner Truth, who remains an icon of inspiration and indomitable spirit, was humbling, inspiring, and overwhelming. I felt a great responsibility upon my shoulders.

For several days after receiving my award, I spent hours immersed, reading Sojourner Truth's narrative. It is a disturbing, upsetting, and emotional account of her life as an enslaved woman and her journey to freedom. If you are not familiar with Sojourner Truth or her life story, I deeply encourage you to learn about her and her phenomenal journey.

The words of Auburn Seminary's motto and "We see you" are exactly why I wrote this book, why I chose twelve legendary women as powerful juju to help us when trials and tribulations test us, when life gets heavy and hard. Twelve is also a sacred, magickal number. It is the number of months in a year and zodiac signs on the wheel.

A Magickal Journey

As if the blessing from Auburn Seminary and the Sojourner Truth Leadership Circle wasn't enough to bring me to my knees in gratitude, in June 2020, I received an email from the Buckland Museum of Witchcraft and Magick.

Yes, indeed. The world-famous Buckland Museum of Witchcraft and Magick, created by the father of American Witchcraft, Raymond Buckland, located in Cleveland, Ohio.

The owner of the collection, Toni Rotonda, whom I have come to call a close, personal friend, came upon my book *Good Juju* at Pantheacon, a convention for the magickal, spiritual community held annually in San Jose, California. It must have been fate for her to come across my book, as she attended the very last Pantheacon.

Pantheacon came to an end in February 2020 after a twenty-six-year run. I never did make it to a Pantheacon conference. I've just had to chalk that up to the flow of divine timing.

However, Toni Rotonda told me that when she came upon my book in the Llewellyn suite, she immediately felt a connection and wanted to reach out to ask if I would consider donating a personal item to the museum!

Before I continue, let's back up a bit. In 2017, Raymond Buckland passed away. Although I had some of his books in my collection, I never had his famous book *Buckland's Complete Book of Witchcraft*, affectionately known as Big Blue, as part of my library. When Mr. Buckland passed away, I kicked myself for not getting it prior to his passing. Getting an edition that was printed before his death would be damn near impossible.

But the magickal ways of the Universe are mysterious. Lo and behold, as I perused the stacks in my favorite used bookstore one afternoon, I came across a copy. I was absolutely thrilled. But the magick didn't stop there. When I opened the book, I saw it was signed! Raymond Buckland had signed the copy to Dave (thank you, Dave, whoever you are). I couldn't believe it. I had a copy of Big Blue, and Mr. Buckland had signed it. Talk about good juju!

Fast-forward to 2020 and receiving the email from the Buckland Museum of Witchcraft and Magick. Not only is it the home of Ray's collection, which includes precious artifacts, but it also has items from Sybil Leek, Aleister Crowley, Janet Farrar, Gerald Gardner, and many other pioneering, inspirational Witches.

To add to this magickal goodness, I learned, per a conversation with Toni Rotonda regarding the history of the collection, that before the collection found its way to Ohio (my birthplace), it was kept and cared for by Reverend Velvet Rieth.

Reverend Velvet was the high priestess and founder of the Pentacle Wiccan Church in Metairie, Louisiana. She was well known in New Orleans for her acts of charity and prison ministry. I had the pleasure of knowing Velvet before she passed away in 2017. She was someone who was very dear to me. Obviously, the wheels of magick had been turning for a while!

I know you're wondering what I donated to the museum. I had several conversations with Toni Rotonda before I settled on an item. I knew the item had to be something precious that mattered to me, something that, when I parted with it, I would deeply miss, yet know when others looked upon it, they, too, would feel and see *me,* and impart some good juju magick.

So, I sent my precious, beloved staff, along with a photograph of myself and these words:

> *My Staff: Blessed in the fires of Beltania, a Pagan Festival held in Colorado, which has now gone into the lands of great festivals, and lives in our memories. Beltania was my first Pagan festival, and it was everything I dreamed of: bonfires, rituals, happy people gathering, ceremonies, camaraderie, and joy.*
>
> *My staff came to me at Beltania. It was created by a great Witch, who left our Earth plane a few years ago. It is unique. There is not another like it.*
>
> *I took my staff to several Colorado Renaissance Faires, where, dressed in medieval garb, we strolled the grounds together and enchanted those of like mind.*
>
> *In December 2019, in preparation for Drumming Up the Sun, which I attended for many years, I added my juju beads [to the staff], tied a red cloth to it in*

honor of Papa Legba, and added bells, which I had lov-
ingly purchased long ago at the Denver March Pow-
wow. With the sounds of bells chiming and the juju
beads shaking in honor of my ancestors and those who
have gone before me, my staff and I climbed the steep
steps at Red Rocks Amphitheatre in Denver, Colorado.
We danced with joy in sacred ceremony as we welcomed
the return of the Sun for the Winter Solstice of 2019.

Little did I know that would be our final ceremony
together. In June 2020, I blessed it, kissed it, and sent
it with love and trust to the Buckland Museum of
Witchcraft and Magick in Cleveland, Ohio, where it
now resides.

May it bring the blessings of good juju to all who
gaze upon it.

I share these words because, as I have been seen, I see *YOU*.
I see you on my Instagram feed, my Twitter and Facebook
newsfeed. I see you trying to make sense of a world that makes
no sense and seems to relish preying on the sensitivities of
others.

I see you crying and praying when horrible tragedies happen, speaking out about being bullied for how you may look
or what you feel. I see you marching in the streets for justice.
I see you demanding accountability for heinous crimes and
murders.

I see you ostracized for standing up for your truth, however
that expresses for you. All these things make me angry. They

upset me. They make me long for examples of strength, hope, and courage. That is why I have written this book. That is why I have chosen Lilith, Frida Kahlo, Marie Laveau, Manman Brijit, Sekhmet, Tituba, Sulis Minerva, Nina Simone, Nancy Wilson, Abundantia, Sybil Leek, and Doreen Valiente to plant seeds of magick, strength, and power in your life.

Always remember, the greatest magick lives within YOU. Even when your cheeks are stained with tears or it feels like the dogs are at your heels, remember, all you need to do is be willing to look within. Summon your courage to practice. Work to develop a strong, magickal practice. Know there is powerful juju at your fingertips to help you, should you choose to call upon it.

So, my dear reader, with these words, we close another chapter in the Good Juju series. It has been my pleasure and great honor to be here with you. I thank you for reading the pages of this book. I truly hope it has been a guide and inspiration to you.

appendix
POWERFUL JUJU PLAYLIST

ALL SONGS ARE AVAILABLE via Apple Music, Pandora, or any other streaming music media. The Powerful Juju Playlist is available on YouTube, iTunes, and Apple Music.

Song Title: **"Couldn't Stand the Weather"**
Artist: Stevie Ray Vaughan
Album: Stevie Ray Vaughan & Double Trouble
Chapter: Introduction

Song Title: **"Darlin' Cory"**
Artist: Amythyst Kiah
Album: Dig
Chapter: Chapter 1: Doing the Work

Song Title: **"Missionary Man"**
Artist: Eurythmics
Album: Ultimate Collection (Remastered)
Goddess: Lilith

Song Title: **"Keep Looking"**
Artist: Sade
Album: Stronger Than Pride
Goddess: Frida Kahlo

Song Title: **"Willow"**
Artist: Joan Armatrading
Album: Joan Armatrading: Greatest Hits
Goddess: Marie Laveau

Song Title: **"Other Side of the Game"**
Artist: Erykah Badu
Album: Baduizm
Goddess: Manman Brijit

Song Title: **"Circle of Life"**
Artist: Tsidii Le Loka, *The Lion King* Ensemble, Lebo M., and
    Faca Kulu
Album: The Lion King: Original Broadway Cast Recording
    (1997)
Goddess: Sekhmet

Song Title: **"Precious"**
Artist: Esperanza **Spalding**
Album: Esperanza
Goddess: Tituba

Song Title: **"Ball and Chain"**
Artist: Janis Joplin
Website: https://youtu.be/X1zFnyEe3nE
Goddess: Sulis Minerva

Song Title: **"Feeling Good"**
Artist: Nina Simone
Album: I Put a Spell on You
Goddess: Nina Simone

Song Title: **"Guess Who I Saw Today"**
Artist: Nancy Wilson
Album: Guess Who I Saw Today: Nancy Wilson Sings …
Goddess: Nancy Wilson

Song Title: **"Forget Me Nots"**
Artist: Patrice Rushen
Album: Forget Me Nots
Goddess: Abundantia

Song Title: **"Time after Time"**
Artist: Cyndi Lauper
Album: She's So Unusual (Remastered)
Goddess: Sybil Leek

Song Title: **"Chasing Pavements"**
Artist: Adele
Album: 19
Goddess: Doreen Valiente

RECOMMENDED READING

Nonfiction

Cornelia Walker Bailey with Christina Bledsoe. *God, Dr. Buzzard, and the Bolito Man.* New York: Anchor Books, Random House, 2000.

This book is a must-read for anyone who is interested in the real lives of African Americans known as the Geechee people, who live on Sapelo Island, Georgia. It is the first-person narrative of Cornelia Walker Bailey, who speaks in a language filled with love for her ancestors, her family, and their spiritual traditions, all who have lived on Sapelo Island since 1803. While reading it, I found myself bursting out in laughter, as I could clearly relate to the way Cornelia talks about Black Folks and some of our ways and traditions. What is also a treat is that the book gives a real account of Folk Magick practices used by the Geechee people on Sapelo Island.

T. F. Earle and K. J. P. Lowe. *Black Africans in Renaissance Europe.* Cambridge, NY: Cambridge University Press, 2005.

Long had I coveted this book on online sites. It is a massive tome, and its price always exceeded the dollars I was willing to spend on a book. But I was drawn to this book for many reasons. I had searched and longed for a testament to Black people during the times of Renaissance Europe, since I love that period of history. I've always felt a kinship to that era of time, but not until this book showed up did I have confirmation at my fingertips. It was a confirmation I needed, because I have spent many years attending the Colorado Renaissance Festival or Pagan festivals where I could count the number of Black Folks in attendance or in costume on one hand. Not only have I attended these festivals and events with glee, but I've also spent many a pretty penny on custom-designed dresses, or Renn garb, as it is affectionately known. It mattered to me to know it was more than just a past-life memory or feeling of déjà vu that my ancestors actually had existed and lived extraordinary lives during these times. As we now say, "Representation matters."

This voluminous book is a master study in art and history. It is filled with pages of black-and-white photos and textual information delineating that which was hidden in plain sight: the story of Black Africans in Renaissance Europe. It is a valuable addition to anyone seeking to expand their knowledge on one of most influential periods of history in Western civilization, and the power of art to tell the story of culture.

Sir James George Frazer. *The Illustrated Golden Bough: A Study in Magic and Religion*. New York: Simon & Schuster Editions, 1996.

The Golden Bough is one of the seminal works on magick and Occultism. Anyone who is a serious student of the Craft has read or will seek to read Sir George James Frazer's *The Golden Bough*. This title is the *illustrated* edition of *The Golden Bough*. Along with the text, the illustrations take the reader deeper into the magickal world of the Occult.

Erica Jong. *Witches*. New York: Harry N. Abrams, 1981.

I bought *Witches* at a Pagan festival. Erica Jong was known for her brilliant book *Fear of Flying*, which spawned an entire movement, inspiring women to get up, get it done, and follow their dreams.

When I saw this book, I immediately knew I had to have it. It is a large book, illustrated magnificently and written so profoundly that I could only read it once because it stirred such deep emotion within me. At times, the illustrations are hard to take, as well as the text. There were moments when I winced as I read it, but I do recommend it. It's a unique work. One that will remain with you long after you have closed its pages.

Charlene Spretnak. *Lost Goddesses of Early Greece: A Collection of Pre-Hellenic Myths*. Boston: Beacon Press, 1984.

I found this book upon the shelf in my all-time favorite used bookstore. I was immediately taken by its golden cover and the word *pre-Hellenic*. Upon looking at the table of contents, I found the names Pandora, Themis, Aphrodite, Demeter, Persephone, Selene, and Hecate. When I thumbed through the pages of the book, I was captivated by the illustrations that accompanied each chapter named for a goddess.

I consider this book a must-read for anyone seriously interested in goddess culture. What makes this book stand out is that it is written by a woman and told from the perspective of how the goddesses may have been seen and honored before men of the Hellenic period put myths to paper.

Fiction

Nnedi Okorafor. *Akata Witch*. New York: Speak, Penguin Random House, 2011.

Nnedi Okorafor! I have fallen in love with this Nigerian American woman's work! Nnedi Okorafor is blowing up the world of science fiction with her titles and her African jujuism! I was so blessed to meet her at a book signing and get a signed copy of this book. She takes you into a world of African rituals, family, beliefs, science fiction, and technology that will stay with you long after you've finished her book. You'll be clamoring to read all the books, stories, and comics that pour forth from her powerful and prolific mind!

Marge Piercy. *Woman on the Edge of Time.* New York: Ballantine Books, 1976.

I love this book! Just looking at the title should be an indication of the fabulous story that lies within. Marge Piercy takes us into a world that only she could have created, dropping us into the life of a Woman of Color who is struggling to make sense of a world that opens to her while she is locked away in a psychiatric ward. Seriously a good read!

Matt Ruff. *Lovecraft Country.* New York: HarperCollins Publishers, 2016.

Twisted and disturbing. Powerful and imaginative. A white dude (as I called him on Twitter and he graciously acknowledged) author takes us into the world of Black Folks, sundown counties, and the Jim Crow era, and he spins a tale so bizarre and scary, I couldn't put it down. It will make you think, upset your mind, and give you many pauses to mull over the past, which is still so gut-wrenchingly present.

Absolutely a great read that was made into an HBO series. Read this book!

Oracle Deck

Fatima Mbodj with Lori Felix. *The New Orleans Oracle Deck.* TheNewOrleansOracleDeck.com.

I love these cards. Fatima Mbodj and illustrator Lori Felix have created one of the most amazing and beautiful oracle decks I have ever beheld! Her prose is uplifting and always gives you a spiritual hug. The paintings for the cards are beautifully illustrated, and if you've ever been to New Orleans, you can feel their authenticity.

If you are looking for a way to touch deeply with the spirit of New Orleans, get this deck! Fatima is a beautiful person I have had the pleasure of meeting several times. She is a visionary, creative force!

Tarot Deck

Jessi Jumanji. *The Afro Tarot.* JessiJumanji.com.

These cards arrived in my life as part of my official alumni status with the Sojourner Truth Leadership Circle, sponsored by Auburn Seminary.

My mouth literally fell open as I gazed at the images. Never had I seen such powerful, strong images depicting people of African ancestry on a tarot card. I became quite emotional as I held the cards in my hand. The images leap from the cards. They touch deep places in your soul, especially if you are an African American, a Black person, or a Person of Color. We need more decks like this one.

I highly recommend this deck as another avenue to open your mind to the infinite possibilities of magickal art, study, and divination.

BiBLiOGrapHy

Books

Buckland, Raymond. *Buckland's Complete Book of Witchcraft*. St. Paul, MN: Llewellyn Publications, 1999.

Calef, Robert. *More Wonders of the Invisible World*. Cambridge, MA: John D. and T. C. Cushing Jr., 1823. Digitized 2007.

Castello-Cortes, Ian. *Desperately Seeking Frida*. Berkeley, CA: Graffito Books, 2018.

Cohodas, Nadine. *Princess Noire: The Tumultuous Reign of Nina Simone*. New York: Pantheon Books, 2010.

Condé, Maryse. *I, Tituba, Black Witch of Salem*. New York: Ballantine Books, 1994.

Cunningham, Scott. *Cunningham's Encyclopedia of Magical Herbs*. St. Paul, MN: Llewellyn Publications, 1998.

De Claremont, Lewis, Frank Householder, Godfrey Spencer, Roy Page Walton, and Catherine Yronwode. *The Secret of Numbers Revealed*. Forestville, CA: Lucky Mojo Curio Company, 2019.

The Doreen Valiente Foundation. *The Charge of the Goddess.* Milton Keynes, UK: Lightning Source UK, 2014.

Dorsey, Lilith. *Orishas, Goddesses, and Voodoo Queens.* Newburyport, MA: Red Wheel/Weiser, 2020.

Farrar, Janet, and Stewart Farrar. *The Witches' Goddess.* Blaine, WA: Phoenix Publishing, 1987.

Glassman, Sallie Ann. *Vodou Visions.* New Orleans, LA: Island of Salvation Botanica, 2007.

Goldschneider, Gary, and Joost Elffers. *The Secret Language of Birthdays.* New York: Penguin Books, 1994.

Grimberg, Salomon. *Frida Kahlo Song of Herself.* New York: Merrell Publishers Limited, 2008.

Heselton, Philip. *Doreen Valiente Witch.* Sussex, England: Doreen Valiente Foundation in association with the Centre for Pagan Studies, 2016.

Leek, Sybil. *Diary of a Witch.* New York: Signet Books, 1968.

Lightfoot, Najah. "Prosperity Magick and the Goddess Abundantia: Create and Work with Money Altars." In *Llewellyn's 2015 Witches' Companion.* Woodbury, MN: Llewellyn Publications, 2015.

Melody. *Love Is in the Earth: A Kaleidoscope of Crystals Updated.* Wheat Ridge, CO: Earth Love Publishing House, 1995.

Morrow Long, Carolyn. *A New Orleans Vodou Priestess, The Legend and Reality of Marie Laveau.* Gainesville, FL: University Press of Florida, 2006.

Pearson, Nicholas. *Stones of the Goddess.* Rochester, VT: Destiny Books, 2019.

Roach, Marilynne K. *Six Women of Salem.* Boston, MA: Da Capo Press, 2013.

Saxon, Lyle. *Fabulous New Orleans.* New York: The Century Company, 1928.

Simone, Nina, and Stephen Cleary. *I Put a Spell on You.* Cambridge, MA: Da Capo Press, 1993.

Valiente, Doreen. *Where Witchcraft Lives.* Copenhagen, Denmark: Whyte Tracks, 2010.

Websites

"Abundantia." Tales Beyond Belief. Accessed January 23, 2020. http://www.talesbeyondbelief.com/roman-gods/abundantia .htm.

"Adele—'Chasing Pavements' LIVE from the Archive." YouTube, July 14, 2011. https://youtu.be/hY_xO1DGfmw.

"Auburn." Auburn Seminary. Accessed January 23, 2020. https://auburnseminary.org.

Badgett, Becca. "Forget-Me-Not Plants—Information on Growing Forget-Me-Nots." Accessed March 4, 2020. https://www.gardeningknowhow.com/ornamental /flowers/forget-me-nots/growing-forget-me-nots.htm.

"Bridget Bishop." Famous American Trials. Accessed March 7, 2020. http://law2.umkc.edu/faculty/projects/ftrials/salem /sal_bbis.htm.

"Chinese Zodiac." China Highlights. Accessed January 23, 2020. https://www.chinahighlights.com/travelguide /chinese-zodiac/.

"The History of the Brotherhood Crusade." The Organization. Accessed March 5, 2020. https://brotherhoodcrusade .org/about-us/.

"Immigration and Emigration: Roman Bath's Celtic Acquisition." BBC. Accessed April 21, 2020. http://www.bbc .co.uk /legacies/immig_emig/england/somerset/article_1.shtml.

"Interview with Sybil Leek, 1 of 3." YouTube, June 10, 2015. https://youtu.be/leYd9Czzylk.

"Interview with Sybil Leek, 2 of 3." YouTube, June 10, 2015. https://youtu.be/uEjzELgLt80.

"Interview with Sybil Leek, 3 of 3." YouTube, June 10, 2015. https://www.youtube.com/watch?v=37-qI1emlnE.

Linder, Douglas O. "The Witchcraft Trials in Salem: An Account." Famous Trials. Accessed June 20, 2021. https:// famous-trials.com/salem/2078-sal-acct.

"*The Lion King* Broadway Cast Takes Over NYC Subway and Sings 'Circle of Life.'" YouTube, August 9, 2014. https:// youtu.be/Qe3SgY5r7zw.

McCallister, Doreen. "Nancy Wilson, Legendary Vocalist and NPR 'Jazz Profiles' Host, Dies at 81." NPR. Last updated December 14, 2018. https://www.nprorg/2018/12/14 /676648086/nancy-wilson-legendaryvocalist-and-npr -jazz-profiles-host-dies-at-81.

"Nancy Wilson." Discogs. Accessed March 5, 2020. https://
www.discogs.com/artist/97917-Nancy-Wilson.

"The Narrative of Sojourner Truth." A Celebration of Women
Writers. Accessed March 30, 2020. https://digital.library
.upenn.edu/women/truth/1850/1850.html.

Norn, Svend, Henrik Permin, Poul R. Kruse, and Edith Kruse.
"[From willow bark to acetylsalicylic acid]." *Dansk medicin-
historisk arbog* 37 (2009): 79–98. https://www.ncbi.nlm.nih
.gov/pubmed/20509453.

"Remembering Nancy Wilson—American Black Journal."
YouTube, December 19, 2018. https://youtu.be/EYJOd
PNuqq4.

"Remembering Nancy Wilson, Singer with Dazzling Style."
One Detroit. Last updated December 17, 2018. https://
www.onedetroitpbs.org/pbs-newshour-remembering
-nancy-wilson-singer-with-dazzling-style/.

"Sulis." A Muse-ing Grace Gallery. Accessed April 21, 2020.
http://www.thaliatook.com/AMGG/sulis.php.

"Sybil Leek." The Witches Almanac. Accessed April 6, 2020.
https://thewitchesalmanac.com/sybil-leek/.

"The Wica." The Wica. Accessed July 18, 2013. https://www
.thewica.co.uk.